'The climate emergency is now well and truly upon us, and at some level we all know it. What this book shows is that accepting that truth is not nihilistic "doomism", but a powerful path to deeper engagement with ourselves and our communities, as citizens alongside one another, not just consumers in isolation from one another. If you're ready to walk that path, this is the book – and the movement – for you.'

Jon Alexander, author of *Citizens* and co-founder
of the New Citizenship Project

'Stopping the climate from breaking down has become a top priority for the UK public – yet many people still feel powerless and political action is far too slow. This brilliant book sets out how climate campaigners and ordinary citizens alike can build a mass movement that translates growing public alarm into a diverse and unstoppable force on the scale that's needed.'

Leo Barasi, author of *The Climate Majority:
Apathy and Action in an Age of Nationalism*

'Resolving the climate crisis will require far greater commitment and action from "ordinary people" than we have seen to date. This book is seeking to stimulate that action. We must all hope that it will be successful, so give it a read and find your route to playing your part in helping to address the greatest challenge of our time.'

Professor Paul Ekins OBE, professor of resources and
environment policy at University College London

'The ambition of the Climate Majority Project – everyone, everywhere, all at once, doing things that are actually effective – is as necessary as it is exciting. We will never get anywhere near climate justice until, as this book sets out, the full truth about our predicament is acknowledged, and widely acted upon. I commend this book to everyone looking to do the only thing that now really matters: acting as if our own lives, and those of our children and their children, and those of our kin across the planet, depend upon it. Which they do.'

Professor Saleemul Huq OBE, director of the
International Centre for Climate Change and Development
and co-author of the IPCC's seminal 1.5°C report

'This fascinating book is needed now more than ever before. We must do more, not only in the Global North but even more in the Global South, where the increasing ravages of ecocide are compelling millions into heightening their various modes of action and to defending their future. The climate majority must be a global majority. The contents of this book, in the context of the crisis that so many are finally waking up to, will justifiably fire people up more vibrantly in advancing our common cause.'

Kofi Klu, co-founder of the Internationalist Solidarity Network

'The only realistic hope for a turnaround in our civilization's disastrous trajectory is for a critical mass of ordinary citizens to push for the deep changes required. This important book offers a thought-provoking new strategy to engage segments of the population who would never normally consider themselves activists in the struggle for a positive future. Demonstrating multiple possible pathways to catalysing a commitment to climate action, it offers a creative alternative to reaching the "climate majority" tipping point that we need.'

Jeremy Lent, author of *The Patterning Instinct*
and *The Web of Meaning*

'Our living world is under unprecedented threat. We must respond now, actively, thoughtfully and in a way that carries the majority with us. The Climate Majority Project is impressively willing to do just this, in a way which is as guided by evidence as it is inspirational, as civil as it is determined. We must rise to the challenge and face the future together. This book shows us how we could truly do this: practical, thoughtful and compassionate, it helps to dismantle the polarities that risk driving us apart. With our help, it really could bring humanity towards that wiser and more "eco-logical" culture which we need if we are to survive.'

Dr Iain McGilchrist, psychiatrist, neuroscience researcher
and author of *The Master and His Emissary*

'No initiative on planet earth is more important than the Climate Majority Project. The ongoing breakdown of our climate is affecting everyone, and everyone needs to do their bit to stop a precarious future becoming cataclysmic. More than anything else, the world needs a mainstream climate movement, and it needs it now. If you care about the future of our planet, and the world your children and grandchildren will inherit, then read this book and be part of the coming wave of citizen climate action. I can guarantee you won't regret it.'

Professor Bill McGuire, professor emeritus of geophysical and climate hazards at University College London and author of *Hothouse Earth: An Inhabitant's Guide*

'Recent freakish floods woke millions up to the crisis facing nature. That awareness means ambitious action for change is inevitable and will become mainstream. Knowing we're part of something wider, something essential, something that is coming through gives us the confidence to play our part. Drawing on both the inspirational and practical aspects of this book, we, the majority, can grow in depth, imagination and power – to become an irresistible force. That is why I strongly commend *The Climate Majority Project* to you.'

Ann Pettifor, economist and author of *The Coming First World Debt Crisis*

'While there will always be a vital role for activism to lead and push the boundaries of what change is possible, now more than ever we need to open the doors to those who care but can never see themselves as activists. This book talks about how we might do that, and this is an important step forward in our collective thinking on how we can protect our home planet.'

Beth Thoren, director of Environmental Action, Patagonia

All proceeds from the sale of this book will support work by the Climate Majority Project to catalyse urgent citizen climate action

THE CLIMATE MAJORITY PROJECT

THE CLIMATE MAJORITY PROJECT

Setting the Stage for a Mainstream, Urgent Climate Movement

Edited by Rupert Read, Liam Kavanagh and Rosie Bell

LONDON PUBLISHING PARTNERSHIP

Published by London Publishing Partnership
www.londonpublishingpartnership.co.uk

ISBN: 978-1-916749-00-9 (pbk)
ISBN: 978-1-916749-01-6 (ePDF)
ISBN: 978-1-916749-02-3 (ePUB)

A catalogue record for this book is
available from the British Library

Typeset in Adobe Garamond Pro by
T&T Productions Ltd, London
www.tandtproductions.com

Printed and bound in Great Britain
by Page Bros

Dedicated to the memory of Saleemul Huq (1952–2023)

Contents

PART IV – DEEPER DIVES

Foreword

We have to reclaim climate as a democratic issue if we are to win the battle for a liveable planet. The simple fact is that only concerted action from governments will be enough to keep the world from increases in average temperature far exceeding 1.5°C (the acceptable limit outlined in the 2015 Paris Agreement). In a democracy, this means that parliaments must back the measures that are essential to get to net zero by 2050.

Understandably, many disillusioned people have given up on the ability of democracies to manage the necessary transition, and at the time of writing, recent government actions in pre-election Britain have poured more fuel on their fire. Whether it's Just Stop Oil or any other group dedicated to direct action, before we attack their methods, we should respect their motivation. Young people in particular recognize the very serious position in which the older generation has left them. We have benefitted from the burning of fossil fuels that is driving climate breakdown, and yet we are failing to take the necessary urgent steps to mitigate the effects of the global heating that we have caused.

It is no longer credible to deny climate change. However, the deniers have now become delayers. They don't want any actions that inconvenience themselves or any of their allies. In fact they still don't really accept the reality of climate change. They ignore the damage it is already causing and discount the devastation that is to come. They are the appeasers, and they must be seen as such. But they will not be defeated by strong-arm tactics. However frustrated we may be at the success of those who, for short-term advantage, delay the changes we must make, we have to win the democratic battle – because it is in parliament that the decisions that matter will be made.

Rupert Read and the Climate Majority Project understand that, and this book is one more step in the campaign to get the moderate majority to stand up and be counted, not only for the sake of our children and our grandchildren, but also for ourselves. The frightening facts of the hottest months ever, the fast-warming sea, the increasing floods, the witheringly hot summers, the disappearance of the sea ice and the rising sea levels should all be a stark reminder of the need for immediate action. It is the world of now and not just that of the future that is threatened.

Only when every elected representative discovers that delay loses votes and appeasement is seen as betrayal will we get the ambitious, committed and consistent government action that we need. This book is a valuable contribution to that end.

Lord Deben, former chair of the UK government's
Committee on Climate Change

Introduction

Rupert Read, Rosie Bell and Liam Kavanagh

A serious climate movement has existed for several decades, but until recently it has stubbornly remained a fringe concern – its members looking on in dismay as a mounting existential threat has lingered on the periphery of public attention. Now, though, a sea change is underway. We are witnessing a critical shift in public climate consciousness, and this book is concerned with how to help catalyse this shift towards the mass citizen action the world now urgently requires to support system change. Throughout society, attitudes to climate are transforming. Too slowly, we may think: too little, too shallow, too late. But time and again we humans are poor predictors of the shape and scale of the change that is to come; blind to what's emerging around us. We'll suggest, in fact, that the sort of climate movement we need to see is not only desirable but close to inevitable. The question is how quickly it can arise.

'We' who answer for these thoughts are a circle of climate activists and strategists – some formerly of Extinction Rebellion (XR) and others from across different areas of social change – who are hoping to offer up a missing piece in the collective response to humanity's biggest crisis. Our collaboration centres on one crucial but often neglected question.

> How can a *majority* of citizens, who now feel concern about the climate and ecological crisis, be supported to turn their anxiety into mass participation in some kind of serious, climate-positive action?

It's a question that many around the world must grapple with if we are to limit ecological catastrophe. We have come to call our own UK-based efforts the Climate Majority Project. This book introduces the thinking behind the project and features a selection of essays from some of the organizers in our own corner of the climate movement, whose dedication and creativity are our hope and inspiration. We do not offer a detailed account of what the climate crisis is, its potential consequences, how it came about or the policies required to 'fix' it. Our focus is instead on the UK climate movement itself: the changing social narratives surrounding citizen action and the means by which to incite the deep collaboration demanded by our times.

Our proposal begins in the gap between awareness and action. Thanks in no small part to the success of the radical climate movement, public awareness of climate threats has rocketed in recent years, as has the appetite for climate-positive leadership and sustainable policy change. *Most* people in the UK now fear climate change and want appropriate action from authorities to reduce emissions and mitigate impacts.[1] But despite people's hopes and expectations, increased visibility and concern has not yet translated into adequate policy or public climate action at anything like the scale needed to drive such policy. It seems unlikely that leaning more heavily upon the same set of protest tactics will change this. If the climate movement does not now turn a significant portion of its energy towards helping activate the citizens it has already influenced, we will not summon enough participation to catalyse needful change within a closing window of opportunity. This book is concerned with the means of that activation. It asks how we may deepen climate awareness to the point that it motivates action of many different kinds. And most importantly, it explores ways to cultivate a mainstream climate movement that supports a diversity of citizens to use their collective power.

A social movement in a big hurry cannot afford to operate on out-of-date assumptions. As such, the climate movement is due a reappraisal of tactics in light of the shifting cultural context. Our position is now both much bleaker and much more promising than that we faced even five years ago. It is bleaker because, despite the efforts of both the radical and moderate factions to spur top-down change from governments 'in time' to avert the worst excesses of warming, it is increasingly clear that time has run out. Climate breakdown is upon us, and meaningful policy solutions are nowhere to be seen. It is more promising, however, because, as a consequence, the distressing signs of dangerous man-made climate change have now penetrated public consciousness to a far greater depth than we typically suppose. This ongoing public awakening together with its backdrop of abject institutional failure present a powerful opportunity to motivate both top-down *and* grassroots action.

In order to grasp this possibility, however, the climate movement must itself embrace a measure of transformation – not least in the fundamental model by which we hope to achieve change. When it comes to climate, our political systems have proven too slow, too short-sighted, too gridlocked and too ensnared in vested interests to prioritize the survival of the people they are meant to serve and to implement change at the rate, scale and depth needed to prevent disaster. Radical climate activism has not succeeded in forcing them to, and yet direct action in this area is often based on the hope that authorities will eventually yield to pressure and deliver. In the coming chapters we will ask what it means for actors in an engaged climate movement not only to 'drive' meaningful change from those at the top, but also to *enact* it wherever in the system they themselves have most power. Importantly, however, far from abandoning a top-down approach, we argue for the kind of citizen action that can, at scale, help build legitimacy for system change. Amid growing awareness of government failures, impressive citizen-led climate initiatives are already arising. As such, the task we outline here is not to design or launch a mass mobilization – it is instead to help create the conditions in which an already emergent movement can become aware of itself, to help facilitate its coordination, and to support its growth.

The approach we will propose is not only tactically different to much climate action that has come before, it is also culturally different. The climate crisis is too vast, complex and multifaceted to be addressed adequately without mass public mobilization. Without an insistent mass mandate at many institutional levels, governments will not make the deep, rapid societal changes that are needed to curb climate breakdown. This movement cannot therefore neglect the requirement of mass *appeal*. While radical groups – XR prominent among them – have succeeded in driving climate action up the public agenda, increased awareness among the general public has not been matched by willingness to participate in those radical groups. With the deepest appreciation for their sacrifice and successes, we must think carefully about whether radical identity may act as a barrier to entry for self-identifying 'ordinary' citizens. And we must consider, with the greatest urgency, what kinds of organizing *can* attract mass participation, leaving prior beliefs about what the climate movement ought to value at the door.

As the Intergovernmental Panel on Climate Change (IPCC) issues increasingly dire warnings, as extreme weather continues to devastate communities, and as floods, wildfires and escalating famine haunt the news cycle, fresh waves of society are jolted into awareness of climate realities. If their options for decisive action in that moment are limited to radical protest groups, then we risk losing the momentum of millions of voices crying out for change. But whereas civil disobedience may be too big an ask for those unmoved by *activism*, many citizens are willing to act if they see a genuinely accessible and effective way to do so. Our aim is not to discover or prescribe one kind of participation that fits all, but rather to help create an on-ramp for the countless diverse possibilities for self-organizing action that constitute a mass-movement-in-waiting. It is to support citizens to recognize that they are not alone in their fears, and that the collective power of their localized initiatives is immense.

At a time when ratcheting up radical tactics might appear the obvious next step for organizers, we call for a focus on mobilizing engagement within this vast 'moderate' territory. Radical groups have made extraordinary progress in shifting public consciousness, and making the most of this shift will require channels for engagement as diverse as the public that wants to act. In time, then, the majority of climate action organizers are likely to come from beyond the traditional 'climate bubble'.

As we will describe, our approach to fostering this activation rests on four simultaneous strands of work that can support people to find motivation, rather than intimidation, in the face of a common threat.

- First, encouraging the ongoing shift in the public story of climate, allowing us to accept that time has run out for a 'safe' climate, and that we can no longer afford to wait for governments to lead the action we need.

- Second, cultivating the communities and practices of support and resilience that can nourish us as we respond to that painful truth together.
- Third, supporting citizens to find the work that is their own to do, and to do it effectively, with maximum leverage. This includes the amplification, scaling and replication both of existing community efforts for mitigation and resilience and of emerging initiatives in workplaces and professions. It also includes countless *new* approaches, collaborations, enquiries and experiments, appropriate to people and place.
- Fourth, promoting a compassionate public conversation that furthers understanding of our predicament and *awareness* of the emergent movement of people, thereby creating channels for action.

While these strands appear as a list, we must stress their *interdependence*: each, we believe, will be necessary to support the others if concern is to turn into motivation.

This might all sound like an extraordinary proposition at any time, let alone in our current geopolitical context. How can people now be expected to cooperate to an unprecedented degree, when by recent appearances we are fatally divided: some of us bent on destruction or dominance of the other as a first priority? Even setting aside the horror of armed conflict, we are accustomed to perceiving our societies as painfully fractured along ideological lines. What will be the basis of cooperation, then? We will argue that a crucial and challenging priority of the Climate Majority Project is to reach beyond the polarization of our times. The threat to all life is the common ground on which we must cooperate – and indeed, as history has shown, shared threats can be naturally unifying to a significant degree.

Whereas many 'issues' in our society have become battlegrounds of individual and group identity, no person or group can successfully dissociate themselves from their environment. Despite the cruel inequity of the extractive behaviours that have brought us to this point, climate breakdown affects everyone. Crucially, however, we will not suggest that it is possible to agree on one shared ideology to underpin climate action. In a diverse society a mass response can only be action based, and its participants must resist the urge to police the motives of others. The response will consist of citizens acting in their own way, wherever they themselves have power. The base is so innately diverse, both politically and culturally, that it could not even be an ambition to agree on our ultimate values before beginning our shared work. In offering these ideas, it is our dearest hope not to deepen factionalism within the climate movement but rather to offer a generative way of looking at our collective challenges that can help coordinate a potentially fragmented base.

In this edited collection of still-emerging ideas, you will encounter a number of different voices, approaching a complex project from different angles, and sometimes overlapping. Treat it as you would any anthology, and dip into those areas that feel most relevant to your own piece of the puzzle. We begin in part I with an introduction to the thinking behind the Climate Majority Project, followed in part II by a discussion of its evolution into the initiative's four-strand Theory of Change. The guest essays in part III feature contributions from organizers of citizen climate action in the UK: the people on the ground who are already realizing the work of the climate majority. Finally, in part IV, three 'deeper dives' reflect on certain core elements of the project's theory of change and on wider challenges relating to the climate movement and societal transformation.

Like all of our predecessors, we are 'building the plane while flying', and our ideas are offered not as a final word but as an exploration – perhaps a provocation. The Climate Majority Project is by no means a finished offering. Its journey has only just begun, and we hope that readers will feel moved to help write its onward story.

NOTES

1   Ipsos Political Monitor (2022). 8 in 10 Britons concerned about climate change – half think net zero target should be brought forward. Report (www.ipsos.com/en-uk/8-10-britons-concerned-about-climate-change-half-think-net-zero-target-should-be-brought-forward).

PART I

MOTIVATION

CHAPTER 1

Shifting awareness: climate consciousness meets the mainstream

Rupert Read and Rosie Bell

ENTERING THE AGE OF CONSEQUENCES: *GOODBYE TO 1.5*

While we are often divided about how to get there, the climate movement is generally interested in human structural and behavioural change that can maintain a stable and biodiverse planet as a basis for life, and in avoiding widespread ecological and civilizational collapse. Since the 2015 Paris Agreement, this goal has become synonymous with limiting the global average temperature rise to 'well below' 2°C, and preferably to 1.5°C. The IPCC was tasked with reporting on the implications of a 1.5°C temperature rise, and in 2018 published a report that was alarming enough to power a new wave of climate action at both the elite and public levels. We can be grateful for the line in the sand that 1.5°C allowed us to draw. This tangible goal facilitated radical climate action through widespread institutional *validation* of the climate emergency. Such legitimacy helped climate to move from fringe concern to headline news, catalysing European Green Deal policy and a wave of related initiatives.

In the intervening years, however, the world's plans for holding atmospheric greenhouse gases within safe limits have tipped from optimism into fantasy. In 2021 the United Nations (UN) warned that countries' combined emissions targets were 'nowhere near' the commitment required to reach Paris 2015 temperature goals, and it projected a rise of 2.7°C by the end of the century on an unchanged trajectory. A disappointing COP26 the same year nonetheless concluded with an unconvincing declaration that '1.5°C is still alive' following an agreement to soften emphasis on phasing out coal (the meaningless term 'phase down' was introduced instead) and leave the necessary measures to be determined at COP27 in 2022. But COP27 did no such thing.[1] Meanwhile, successive IPCC reports repeatedly postpone our last best chance. In 2022 it was 'now or never' for 'deep and immediate cuts' to emissions, without which chances of hitting the target were estimated at less than 33%.[2] With the emissions curve still refusing to bend, 2023's synthesis report[3] was widely described as a 'final warning': on current trajectories, the remaining carbon budget will be used up before the end of the decade. And without said 'deep and immediate' cuts, mitigation pathways depend on 'overshoot': allowing average warming to exceed 1.5°C, potentially for decades, before bringing it back under control through theoretical future technology such as direct air capture.[4]

While we wait for the requisite technologies to be invented and deployed at scale, carbon emissions continue to climb, on a horrifying 'burn now, pay later' trajectory.[5] Meanwhile, without ceremony or public acknowledgement, our relationship with the idea of a 'safe limit' has transformed. From being an ambitious target at which to direct sincere global effort, the 1.5°C goal has become a mirage, no longer rooted in meaningful science but in wishful thinking. Those climate experts who still publicly assert that this target will be met say so for no better reason than *because it must*. Clinging to what may be technically possible while avoiding deeper analysis of current political impossibilities, we remain cocooned by this narrative of future salvation.

In May 2023 the World Meteorological Organization issued a groundbreaking statement that the world will almost certainly begin to exceed the 1.5°C average threshold within the next few years.[6] In June 2023 the 1.5°C 'limit' was breached for the first time in the northern hemisphere's summer months, and at the time of writing extreme ocean temperatures and the onset of a strong El Niño event increase the likelihood that the temperature rise will exceed 1.5°C for longer periods.[7] We should be under no illusion about the seriousness of this moment of failure. It will be remembered by future generations as a defining moment, but its implication remains to be determined. On the one hand, there is now a crucial chance to publicly acknowledge that our politically agreed 'safe' target has been missed, and then to act accordingly from a place of realism. The alternative is to go on procrastinating. To load 1.5, then perhaps 1.6, then the next best target and the next, with increasingly far-fetched hopes until they too are lost. Shifting the goalposts inch by inch, we can slide steadily into catastrophe while still maintaining that future technology will save us. As Marc Lopatin discusses in chapter 12, the effect of this eternally flexible 'last warning' is to limit public consciousness and action on climate, forever stalling the mass outcry that could actually underpin a mandate for change. We will outline the need for a shift in the public narrative on climate – a necessary if not a sufficient condition for citizen action. Such a shift means saying goodbye to our belief that climate safety will be achieved just in time. We have entered the age of consequences: the time is now five *past* midnight.

THE EVOLVING CASE FOR A MASS MOVEMENT

To quote UN secretary-general Antonio Guterres, climate action is needed 'on all fronts – everything, everywhere, all at once'.[8] Crucially, as we will argue, this must now include the majority of citizens. Without an insistent mass mandate at many civil and institutional levels, governments will not make the deep, rapid changes that are needed to avert catastrophic damage. This task demands nothing less than a mass climate movement: a wave of collective will for societal change on a scale rarely witnessed before.

'Crisis' is the word we have settled on for the complex conditions amounting to climate breakdown and ecological destruction, and recent insistence on this upgrade from the weaker 'climate change' is a step in the right direction. However, this does not deter the public assumption that here is just one more problem among many: a specific, boundaried issue within a larger system whose stability remains independently intact. Humanity at large may choose to ignore a butter crisis, a fuel crisis or a refugee crisis without expecting global societal structures – or planetary ecosystems – to break down. Not so the climate crisis, which, without adequate action, may render all other issues irrelevant. Climate and ecology is not an 'issue' at all, it is our very basis of life. As H. J. Schellnhuber has said, 'If we don't solve the climate crisis, we can forget about the rest.'[9]

By the same token, the rules informing theories of change in the climate movement are different to those underpinning single-issue activism. For example, whereas civil rights movements have traditionally pushed for specific political changes that primarily affect specific groups in particular locations, climate activism seeks to drive global systems change.[10] An adequate response entails myriad interacting policy changes across diverse sectors, coordinated in a far-sighted manner that accounts for social consequences and avoids creating worse injustice than it solves. To propel such wholesale transformation of the status quo in the short time remaining to us – and in the face of fearsome vested interests and inertias – vast buy-in across society is required.

The level of aligned intergovernmental intervention, financial investment, public support, lifestyle change, sacrifice and cooperation that it will take, and the mass citizen backing needed to realize it, is not, as we might first think, unimaginable. It is not even unprecedented. Whether painfully present or fading in the national memory, every country has its proud stories of pulling together to achieve the impossible in the face of annihilation. Indeed, as far back as 2008, senior UN figures were calling for the international community to adopt a 'war-footing' on climate, to avoid both erasing development gains in poorer nations and wider ripple effects, including mass migration and refugee flows, ultimately impacting security on a global scale.[11]

Echoed by many advocates and activists, this metaphor of war is perhaps the only concise image that comes close to illustrating the scale of catastrophe, destruction and threat to life that is currently unfolding and the scale of response called for to address it in time. However, few realities are as tangible and galvanizing as the threat of physical harm – we are physiologically attuned to respond urgently to immediate, embodied threats to survival. Conversely, while we may learn factually about the dangers of anthropogenic climate change, its slow-moving, uncertain and abstract nature means that we do not *experience* it as an immediate threat[12] – not without a greater effort of imagination and empathy at least. So, it has taken a perceptible increase in climate tragedy to make a dent in mainstream awareness, particularly in the West, where responsibility for driving climate decline is gravely disproportionate to the consequences felt. This slowness to grasp our peril is compounded by a public narrative that suggests that authorities have the matter in hand (see chapter 12).

ENGAGING THE MASSES: EXTINCTION REBELLION'S FOOT IN THE DOOR

The urgent need to engage mass society in response to the true severity of climate threat has been the basis of stark messaging and radical tactics from the protest movement Extinction Rebellion (XR) since its launch in 2018. The group's strategists did not expect a majority simply to fall in step behind a new, radical group – rather, based on historical precedent, they predicted that a more modest following would contribute a tipping point for larger success. XR's founders set a target of mobilizing 3.5% percent of the population, based on the work of political scientist Erica Chenoweth. Research by Chenoweth and Stephan suggests that campaigns that mobilize at least 3.5% of the population in sustained, nonviolent protest are likely to succeed in their aims.[13] As some have noted, the research in question applies mainly to campaigns to overthrow autocratic governments,[14] and treating it as a pillar of strategy in a very different context far from guarantees the desired result. Furthermore, focus on this figure of 3.5% risks downplaying the other related factors contributing to a tipping point. For example, a protest movement must consider not only its active membership but also the importance of influencing and aligning with wider public attitudes. Where a movement is successful, it's likely that the 3.5% represents the active tip of an iceberg of tacit public support[15] (as in the Arab Spring movements, on which much of Chenoweth's research was based).

Despite extraordinary ongoing efforts and achievements, XR did not gather the support necessary to see its demands met, even by its own optimistic estimates. Three point five percent of the UK population is two million people. In its October 2019 'rebellion' XR doubled its participation, and it was successful in attracting sympathy in response to government crackdowns. But participation in rebellions still peaked at around 6,000 people: 0.3% of the forces that XR thought necessary. The tactically moderate 'Grief March' midway through the October 2019 rebellion attracted 10,000–12,000 participants, while 60,000 people attended 'The Big One' in April 2023: a great achievement, but still a minute fraction of Chenoweth's modest target.

We may suggest reasons why support for XR reached a ceiling but we can never be certain. While a number of later actions[16] were perceived as too extreme, denting public support with the help of hostile media, there is no guarantee that without them the movement would have continued to grow. There may be a natural flattening to the curve of any protest movement's growth, governed by factors like diminishing novelty and newsworthiness, and by a finite quantity of 'low-hanging fruit' in terms of activists who are ready to engage.

Six years after XR set out to awaken the masses, and with climate breakdown having worsened in the meantime, no mass citizen *activism* is yet in evidence. However, the undeniable fact that momentum has slowed so many miles short of the line is not a cause for despair. Neither, as we will argue, is it a case for throwing energy behind further efforts to radicalize a hesitant public. More of the same is not the only way to make good the intense investment of recent years. Instead we may acknowledge that XR prepared the ground for the very different, vastly larger wave of citizen *action* that comes next. Amid a tipping point in public awareness, precipitated by a decade of mounting crisis, societal attitudes towards climate have shifted dramatically, with a majority of citizens now reporting some level of concern.[17] What follows is a case for cultivation of this legacy – for making actual what XR made possible.

A PUBLIC AWAKENING

It's important to stress that this work does not seek to reproach the radical climate activism that was so transformative in 2019. XR's achievements have been nothing short of phenomenal. So much so that it is worth reminding ourselves that as recently as 2018 – despite the long-term efforts of the Green Party and various large non-governmental organizations (NGOs) – there was *no* widespread public conversation on climate or ecology. Public awareness was virtually non-existent, and the BBC was still routinely hosting climate denialists in the interest of 'balanced reporting'.

Beginning in 2016, however, a confluence of factors ultimately brought about a sea change. The first of these was intensifying extreme weather: the undeniable succession of hurricanes, wildfires and typhoons tracking though the news and, painfully slow off the mark, the acknowledgement of climate impacts in commentary. Also critical in shifting the dial were the popular School Strike for Climate movement, initiated by Greta Thunberg, and the release of *Climate Change – The Facts* by David Attenborough and BBC One in April 2019. But in the UK at least, by far the most influential factor was XR's execution of a highly effective strategy, including the world-first achievement of mass, non-violent direct action on climate and ecology. The group's key demands were not met in their entirety; however, significant concessions were extracted from Theresa May's outgoing government. Opinion polls demonstrated a surge of support for meaningful climate action, and the UK parliament responded by declaring a (symbolic) climate and environmental emergency. Surprisingly, it also legislated a commitment to reaching net zero carbon emissions by 2050 and created a climate citizen's assembly, albeit one lacking in significant decision-making power.

Here we are less interested in symbolic gestures from government, however, than we are in the shift in public consciousness that made those gestures strategically appealing to those in power. Thanks in part to XR's actions, a previously marginalized climate movement has been widely legitimated, and the terms of debate on climate breakdown have undergone a fundamental shift in the public conversation.

THE RADICAL FLANK EFFECT

Explicit in XR's design was the psychology of its relationship to the preexisting environmental movement. Drawing on historical precedent, XR set out to become a 'radical flank' to existing groups. In both aims and tactics it would be bolder and go further than the Green Party, Friends of the Earth and Greenpeace,[18] demanding much more from government and regularly pushing the boundaries of disruptive behaviours associated with climate action.

Social movement literature suggests a radical flank *effect* to explain the success of social movements whose first wave of activity is 'outflanked' by escalating civil disobedience from a more radical faction of the same movement. While sharing the light of attention generated by increased disruption, the once-outlying goals and behaviour of the existing movement may begin to appear modest and reasonable by comparison. The 'moderate' cause therefore attracts more resources, and decision makers are presented with an apparent choice: sit down and negotiate to deliver the goals of moderates, or deal with tactical escalation (and potentially increased demands) by radicals.[19]

Importantly, on this account, radical and moderate are not absolute values; rather they continually redefine each other as their referents shift within public perception. During the 1960s, for example, the American civil rights movement was advanced not only by increased radicalism from within – including children's marches – but also by the rise of more hardline black nationalist flanks. Famously, Martin Luther King Jr, himself previously seen as a radical, exploited this contrast when negotiating with the Kennedy administration – urging the common sense of dealing fairly with his own associates, the better to defuse more militant efforts by Malcolm X and other (relative) radicals. Around the same time, reformist feminism benefited from a similarly legitimating effect thanks to the rise of radical feminism.[20] Wherever this effect is in evidence, pressure groups once seen as radical in the public eye become 'moderate' not by shifting their own stance or tactics but in relation to the behaviours of a new radical flank.

XR's strategy was not limited to the radical flank effect: the rebels energetically strove to succeed on their own terms and to see specific, ambitious demands met. Nonetheless, their biggest victory to date has been to legitimate the climate movement at large, helping once-radical climate concern to become common sense and driving urgent action on ecology up the public policy agenda. Even the later XR actions that dented public sympathy tended to create a retroactive narrative of legitimacy around their own earlier tactics, which were reinterpreted as mild and within the bounds of decency after the group was perceived as having 'gone too far'. By late 2019, when public approval had begun to sour around controversies such as the Canning Town DLR protest,[21] even right-wing commentators were prone to qualified outbursts of sympathy with the environmental cause, often restricting censure to XR's distastefully radical image and tactics. When, without a whiff of irony, the *Daily Telegraph* letters page begins 'SIR – We are all rightly concerned about climate change, but ...',[22] you may be reassured that your 'ineffective, self-defeating methods'[23] have in fact found their mark.

SHIFTING THE WINDOW

The 'Overton window' theory of political possibility is a helpful lens for radical flank tactics. Joseph Overton characterized the range of political ideas the public is willing to consider and accept as a 'window' – outside the frame are ideas that are too extreme or obscure by current standards, and towards the centre are those ideas that become policy.[24] It's the role of advocates and social movements not just to place direct pressure on decision makers, but to shift or expand this window of public opinion in the direction of their own marginalized cause – sometimes gradually, sometimes rapidly.[25] As formerly unthinkable ideas become acceptable to society, policymakers gravitate to the shifted centre and enact change. That the most extreme demands remain outside the window does not signify failure: the sought-for shift is not all-or-nothing but rather along a spectrum of acceptability. In such a way, XR helped shift the range of public debate to include climate, and policy followed – albeit insufficient.

Overton's window is often invoked as a rationale for extreme tactics or policies, but in the conventional understanding at least, it offers an overly simplistic theory of change. For one thing, the image of a window moved along a track can suggest that changing the public agenda is a linear process, driven by external pressure. Unavoidably, this model somewhat flattens the complexities of social transformation. A shift does not come about only because we force it to, but as a result of our actions at a particular time, within a wider set of systemic conditions. We can't just campaign for another avalanche.

JUST PUSH HARDER?

In light of the successes gained by XR despite relatively low active participation, there is perhaps a natural temptation to push harder – to throw the climate movement's weight behind more extreme radical flank activity in order to shift the window even further and drive more effective policy. In the wake of XR, groups like Insulate Britain and Just Stop Oil have re-energized efforts in the UK's radical climate movement, making headlines with a range of soup-throwing, snooker-foiling, motorway-blocking tactics and clear, insistent messaging: the climate demands attention. Similarly, XR has threatened to return to civil disobedience following its more moderate, movement-building efforts with 'The Big One' in early 2023.

Our thesis is *not* necessarily that this approach doesn't help – although we see no good reason to expect that repeating our actions within a new set of conditions is likely to replicate recent large-scale successes,[26] especially now that XR's initial wave of growth and widespread popularity has demonstrably plateaued. Citizen approval around recent radical actions has been mixed at best, and Suella Braverman's Home Office has responded to escalation in recent years with a range of draconian legislative measures empowering police to restrict protest behaviour in the UK, with significant polling support for measures regarding disruption. Importantly, though, we are not concerned here with the question of how effective continued radical action can be in shifting public attitudes. Rather, we urge that, regardless of any potential to further shift the window, there now exists an urgent need *to follow through on the gains already made by radical efforts.* Shifting opinion is a strategic goal, but it is not an end in itself – this is the territory of thought, not action. If we all remain preoccupied with moving the dial, we run a very real risk of wasting the fruits of radical successes.

In social systems as in biological systems, a decisive shift such as the one we have witnessed since 2018 marks the beginning of a new phase of life – an environment rich with possibility. Within this landscape is a mass-movement-in-waiting; not thousands but millions of newly awakened citizens beginning to ask, 'What can I do?' The climate movement must now answer them without demanding the impossible. As we will discuss, the movement we hope to catalyse is one that supports this concerned 'climate majority' to find what is theirs to do. One that not only magnifies the pressure on decision makers to act, but itself becomes a vehicle for both mitigation and adaptation.

NOTES

1   At the time of writing, the petrostate-hosted COP28, presided over by the CEO of UAE's national oil company, promises no better outcome and, probably, domination of fossil fuel interests.

2   IPCC (2022). The evidence is clear: the time for action is now. We can halve emissions by 2030. Newsroom post, 4 April (www.ipcc.ch/20 22/04/04/ipcc-ar6-wgiii-pressrelease/).

3   IPCC (2023). AR6 synthesis report: climate change 2023. Report (www.ipcc.ch/report/ar6/syr/).

4   Boehm, S., and Schumer, C. (2023). 10 big findings from the 2023 IPCC Report on Climate Change. World Resources Institute (www.wri. org/insights/2023-ipcc-ar6-synthesis-report-climate-change-findings)

5   Dyke, J., Watson, R., and Knorr, W. (2022). Climate scientists: concept of net zero is a dangerous trap. *The Conversation*, 22 April (https:// theconversation.com/climate-scientists-concept-of-net-zero-is-a-dang erous-trap-157368).

6   Copernicus (2023). Tracking breaches of the 1.5°C global warming threshold. News (https://climate.copernicus.eu/tracking-breaches-15 0c-global-warming-threshold).

7   World Meteorological Organization (2023). World Meteorological Organization declares onset of El Niño conditions. Press Release, 4 July (https://public.wmo.int/en/media/press-release/world-meteorol ogical-organization-declares-onset-of-el-ni%C3%B1o-conditions).

8   UN Audiovisual Library (2023). Gutteres IPCC report (www.unmulti media.org/avlibrary/asset/3022/3022200/).

9   Professor Hans Joachim Schellnhuber quoted in Roberts, J. (2019). 'I would like people to panic' – top scientist unveils equation showing world in climate emergency. European Comission/Horizon (https://ec .europa.eu/research-and-innovation/en/horizon-magazine/i-would-pe ople-panic-top-scientist-unveils-equation-showing-world-climate-em ergency).

10   Ahmed, N. (2019). The flawed social science behind Extinction Rebel-lion's change strategy. *Resilience*, 31 October (www.resilience.org/stor ies/2019-10-31/the-flawed-social-science-behind-extinction-rebellions -change-strategy/).

11   UN General Assembly (2008). Battle against climate change calls for 'war footing', deputy secretary-general says as general assembly holds follow-up to February thematic debate. Press Release, 8 July (https:// press.un.org/en/2008/ga10725.doc.htm).

12   See, for example, Van Vugt, M., Griskevicius, V., and Schultz, P. W. (2014). Naturally green: harnessing Stone Age psychological biases to foster environmental behavior. *Social Issues and Policy Review* 8(1):1–32 (https://doi.org/10.1111/sipr.12000).

13   Chenoweth, E., and Stephan, M. J. (2011). *Why Civil Resistance Works: The Strategic Logic of Nonviolent Conflict*. Columbia University Press.

14   See, for example, Matthews, K. R. (2020). Social movements and the (mis)use of research: Extinction Rebellion and the 3.5% rule. *Inter-face* 12(1):591–615 (https://commonslibrary.org/wp-content/uploads/ Interface-12-1-Matthews.pdf).

15   See, for example, Isabel Bramsen quoted in Robson, D. (2019). The '3.5% rule': how a small minority can change the world. *BBC Future*, 14 May (www.bbc.com/future/article/20190513-it-only-takes-35-of -people-to-change-the-world).

16   Read, R., and Alexander, S. (2020). *Extinction Rebellion: Insights from the Inside*. Simplicity Institute.

17   DESNZ Public Attitudes Tracker: net zero and climate change (Spring 2023; https://assets.publishing.service.gov.uk/government/uploads/sys tem/uploads/attachment_data/file/1164127/desnz-pat-spring-2023- net-zero-and-climate-change.pdf).

18   Illustrative of the intention to operate as a radical flank was XR's occu-pation of Greenpeace's headquarters before trying to occupy or block government offices.

19 See, for example, Haines, H. H. (1984). Black radicalization and the funding of civil rights: 1957–1970. *Social Problems* 32(1):31–43.

20 See, for example, Freeman, J. (1975). *The Politics of Women's Liberation: A Case Study of an Emerging Social Movement and Its Relation to the Policy Process.* Addison-Wesley Longman.

21 In October 2019, action on the Docklands Light Railway went ahead despite overwhelming opposition from within the movement. Some violence ensued, and extensive negative press coverage left the movement's reputation badly tarnished.

22 Letters to the editor. *The Telegraph*, 10 October 2019 (www.telegraph.co.uk/opinion/2019/10/09/lettersextinction-rebellions-disruptive-tactics-killing-public/).

23 Foges, C. (2019). Climate activists need Middle England allies. *The Times*, 7 October (https://www.thetimes.co.uk/article/climate-activists-need-middle-england-allies-mlfs56rbx).

24 On Overton's model, developed and popularized by Joseph Lehman, the spectrum of political ideas along which the window moves ranges from less to more free with regard to government intervention; however, the model is commonly used to describe other spectra (e.g. left/right) or specific issues.

25 See, for example, Lehman, J. (2010). An introduction to the Overton window of political possibility. Mackinac Center for Public Policy (www.mackinac.org/12481).

26 According to Rune Ellefson, radical flank effect research has too often ignored the conditions under which particular radical flank effects occur and failed to acknowledge that radical flank effects might change over time, producing different, yet interrelated, outcomes: an initial positive radical flank effect might subsequently be reversed as a conflict drags on. See Ellefsen, R. (2018). Deepening the explanation of radical flank effects: tracing contingent outcomes of destructive capacity. *Qualitative Sociology* 41:111–133 (10.1007/s11133-018-9373-3). Arguably, both Insulate Britain and Just Stop Oil have run this risk.

CHAPTER 2

Come as you are: towards a new wave of citizen climate action

Rupert Read and Rosie Bell

'MODERATE FLANK' STRATEGY

If the climate movement's radical flank has succeeded by reframing and normalizing its moderate predecessors, we will propose that a (new) 'moderate flank' can succeed by making the most of this shift in public consciousness to power transformation at scale. 'Moderate' activity has the potential to drive massive political change precisely because the *majority* of latent energy for climate action now lies in moderate territory, with newly concerned citizens who are still not attracted to participating in radical tactics.[1] Mobilizing this energy does *not* mean, however, reverting to pre-XR climate tactics and hoping for different results. While older large NGOs such as Greenpeace and Friends of the Earth are recast as moderate by the recent shift, the success of radical action has opened up imaginative space for vastly more diverse channels of re-energized citizen action, inviting widespread innovation. Here we offer not an exhaustive plan, but rather a frame for understanding both the emergent climate action made possible by the radical flank and its potential to underpin a mass movement: the climate majority.

You will notice the repeated scare quotes around the word 'moderate', and we must be careful to avoid several potential misunderstandings. Moderate flank strategy should not be seen as advocating against the radical flank, or as trying to steer the political agenda back towards moderate aims or values in an ideological tug of war. Nor does it seek less ambitious change, or work in any way to counteract the radical movement. Rather it begins the work of imagining what is needed to mobilize a concerned population that will never identify as radical, nor even in most cases as 'activist' (see chapter 14). Moderate in tactics rather than aims or outlook, it includes in the first instance a greatly widened, deliberate and accessible climate *conversation*, with messaging that meets people where they are, in a language that is meaningful to them. Only in such a space can people come to terms with their difficult reality and discover their own work to do, together. The work itself entails every imaginable initiative for proactive mitigation, adaptation and collective bargaining that is *more* transformative than the usual menu of recycling and occasional voting and *less* demanding than seeking arrest through full-scale civil disobedience. Imagine looking through Overton's window to see a colourful garden growing into every available inch of the space behind.

This living image is the starting point for convening an inclusive climate majority. Among its founding principles is the understanding of the ecological movement itself as an ecology, and the need to encourage diverse climate action to grow wherever it can take root. A true majority movement cannot be centralized in terms of ideology or prescribed action. It must be distributed, yet consciously joined up; founded upon healthy relationships between distinct, complementary organisms. The risks it takes and the resources it requires are also distributed, making the whole system fundamentally more resilient than a movement that lives and dies by its central ideology, its flagship tactics and its fickle PR success.

THE NEXT BIG THING WILL BE ... *A LOT OF THINGS*

The activity we describe is already emerging in places where citizens have power, such as professional sectors, workplaces, businesses and local communities. It takes diverse forms, informed by citizens' particular strengths, vulnerabilities and leverage within current systems. It interacts with the system it seeks to change at all sorts of levels:

building awareness, influencing decision makers *and* directly enacting needful change (see chapter 4).

A growing body of groundbreaking groups and platforms is already focused on active change – from community groups retrofitting homes[2] and towns working towards net zero,[3] to influential figures in law, business and finance[4] lobbying for ambitious climate policy and modelling climate leadership from within their own firms. Many thousands of such collaborations are needed to realize the possibility of an active climate majority, and it is our job to help them to multiply and connect with each other – and with as many willing hands as possible.

To be clear, we do not imagine ourselves to be the founders or builders of such an ecology: we can only do everything in our power to create conditions that support it, and to help an emerging movement to become aware of itself. This awareness is key: the capacity to drive change at many levels comes from the aggregated power of citizens, motivated by the understanding that their initiatives are part of a much larger wave. Such an understanding can empower ever more willing people to engage in meaningful climate action; in turn showing leaders that they have a mass mandate for extraordinary measures.

LIMITATIONS OF A RADICAL/MODERATE DISTINCTION

The term 'moderate flank' was gently retired in the process of founding a public-facing organization around this core idea. Indeed, the word 'moderate' can mislead, not least because it fails to do justice to the ultimate aims of this project, which include the same degree of deep societal transformation as explicitly 'radical' climate projects, albeit by more accessible means.

For example, the work of aligned groups such as the Community Climate Action Project and Transformative Adaptation is based on an understanding that significant damage is inevitable, and that adaptation is therefore unavoidable and must be embraced (as well as adequately defined). On this approach, the radical thing is reckoning with reality. It is too late to somehow force a swift, smooth transition to a long-term viable civilization: there is some damage we will not fix, and we will not achieve change overnight. To accept this – to slow down and base our actions on what we *can* achieve – means facing up to grief, fear and disappointment.

Similarly, when considering what we really want from 'radical' action, we ought to include the kind of literally *direct* action that does not outsource responsibility for change to derelict higher powers. For example, working directly to enact change in businesses and workplaces, or to build community resilience on the ground, circumvents the protest model. This move 'from resistance to insistence',[5] from protest to positive action, may be seen as transformative in ways that go beyond non-violent direct action, while remaining more accessible to large, non-radical segments of the population (see also chapter 14). At the same time, it can apply pressure on authorities to align with visibly shifting public opinion.

THE BIG TENT

A sense of belonging to the broad-based climate movement must not be made conditional on commitment to any political agenda – progressive, conservative or otherwise. A climate movement big enough to succeed will by definition be a broad coalition. If it fails to include a majority of the population, it will fail outright. It can't be fulfilled by radical approaches alone, because the majority now primed for engagement is constituted by elements of society with little interest in radical behaviour or identity. These recent converts have not previously demonstrated any enthusiasm for civil disobedience, and while this may change if societal conditions deteriorate severely, it will not happen any time soon. So far, so uncontroversial: every movement has plenty of roles to be filled by individuals who do not fancy glueing themselves to the pavement. However, securing the cooperation of those individuals also requires a movement in which they feel represented – or, at a bare minimum, not unwelcome. Accordingly, XR set out in its earliest incarnation to 'go beyond politics', placing inclusivity at the heart of its flagship citizens' assembly policy. But the group did little else to avoid projecting a political culture associated with the radical left or with anarchism in the UK and elsewhere, thereby opting, in a sense, to remain marginal.

The concerned majority is distributed across a wide political spectrum. Beyond climate's 'usual suspects' on the progressive left, many incline towards the centre and the right: a sincere conservatism that is serious about preserving and protecting the living world.[6] Some will already feel alienated or chastised by the cultural and linguistic codes of radical social justice movements. The stakes are now too high to risk excluding those people. As such, in convening a politically effective climate majority there can be no insistence on a single ideology or set of values, and no group should present itself as a gatekeeper for the movement at large. For example, while it is certainly the case that many of the changes the world needs are functionally inseparable from matters of international equity and justice, and while intersectionality and decolonization are pillars of well-known approaches to climate action, it can't be the task of the climate movement to tell its members how to feel about those ideas or which of them to prioritize. Excluding citizens who are not signed up to them imposes a disastrous cap on participation.

A critical difference must be stressed between advocating an inclusive movement and promoting moderate ideology. We do not suggest that a true political neutrality can ever be reached – far less that it is to be desired. The Climate Majority Project doesn't lay claim to the 'view from nowhere'.[7] Quite the opposite, in fact: it advocates making space for every willing body without passing judgement. *Come as you are.* Nothing about this approach entails returning to a regime of imagined 'normality', where the voice and visibility of marginalized groups or views is erased. A genuinely inclusive movement has space for those whose first priority is intersectional social justice as well as those whose principal motivation is love of nature, for example, or a sense of heritage and posterity. It will include those who are motivated primarily by their own children's needs, or those of their grandchildren or their community, as well as those whose ethics encompass vulnerable communities across the globe.

It is likewise important to highlight that the inclusivity of the climate majority is not a case of gathering everyone under one big umbrella and moving as one. While in developing this project we have often been asked how we propose to 'include' everyone, we emphasize that the diversity of the climate movement is not ours to include or even to invite. Diversity is an innate quality of a movement that is broad-based and distributed. It may be encouraged, however, through messaging that does its best to avoid projecting a narrow set of cultural qualities.

As mentioned above, the diversity of such a coalition is the foundation of its resilience and efficacy. The living systems we seek to protect teach us that monoculture is unnatural, depleting, inefficient and prone to wholesale collapse. Flourishing ecologies thrive symbiotically: interdependent organisms effecting compatible processes and fully realizing the space available, nourishing each other in ways that would be impossible to imagine by analysing one organism in isolation. The same is true of the mass climate movement that is waiting to form. The climate crisis and its psychosocial roots reach into diverse corners of lived experience. Every person's relationship with the crisis, including their capacity to act, is shaped by a unique set of circumstances.[8] A one-size-fits-all movement cannot respond appropriately to this kind of distributed threat, or make the most of its opportunities.

At this pivotal historic moment it can't be emphasized too strongly that the only healthy climate movement is one that is *inclusive of left, right and centre*. Society's current patterns suggest that the alternative may be more sinister than we typically imagine. The mechanics of polarization that pervade our most important social issues entail that as climate concern truly becomes a mainstream issue, the climate movement itself will be susceptible to polarization. What we must avoid is not just the already-familiar situation where climate is perceived as a left-wing issue, with voices on the the right tending to minimize the problem and dampen solutions. Rather, it is the scenario where, by attracting moderate citizens who feel excluded by a 'radical left' movement, a powerful alternative climate movement emerges, directing its energy towards anti-democratic, right-wing climate politics. Such a force could deploy populist strategies to divert political energy towards climate 'solutions' devoid of equity, fixated on defensive adaptation and hostile to other countries. The very real risk of driving newly awakened citizens towards eco-authoritarian or even eco-fascist groups gives us a powerful incentive to resist polarizing forces with all of our energy.

In avoiding promoting any single ideology, we must be careful not to suggest that climate and ecological breakdown can be neatly (and *truthfully*) addressed without a majority of people ever confronting the deeper systemic conditions that have brought it about. These conditions include, for example, a widespread unawareness of our interconnection with nature, underpinning environmental destruction, consumerism, fixation on economic growth and desires for dominance over others and nature.[9] And while it is tempting to think that climate change can be 'fixed' by technology, the challenge of curbing biodiversity loss – our damage to the web of life – presents even greater challenges to our current ways of living. To give deep systemic factors their due generates a tension: to do so has traditionally been the territory of 'progressives' and so carries an ideological flavour that can risk alienating more mainstream groups. However, a broad-based movement to create *viable* responses to ecological breakdown will inevitably challenge the core mindsets responsible for the systems and symptoms we wish to change.

This tension is eased, we hope, by emphasizing the actions we can all work on, together, while we contemplate deeper questions of system change. As chapter 3 will discuss, what we can most effectively offer is an accessible route to conversation and pragmatic climate action grounded in relatable concerns. The communities of support and the processes of collaboration that arise around these efforts may then become a safe container for deeper dialogue, and for a wholly voluntary journey of learning about more 'distant' causes of the problems felt locally. To insist on a particular attitude to these matters at the outset would too easily exclude those who might otherwise be willing to take that journey. Conversely, within communities that are already cooperating in common cause, there are good reasons to expect (and ways to support) deepening understanding around more systemic issues (see also chapter 4).

CREATING CONDITIONS FOR RECONNECTION

Polarizing dynamics are currently so entrenched that it is possible to forget that we are allowed to reject them – that beyond the digitally manipulated stories of 'us versus them' that fracture our communities and causes, there are fundamental values that we share with those around us. As groups like Parents for Future emphasize, the imperative to protect what we love in the face of existential threat is certainly a profound basis for collaboration.[10] At all times our lives are interwoven through modes of belonging that cross-cut political boundaries. We share identity as parents, kin and caregivers. As workers. As members of communities, grounded in place.

This view may risk sounding naive to some: 'Can't we all just get along?' And of course we cannot simply call for unity and expect it to appear. Such ambitions demand deep commitment to creating conditions for mutual respect and collaboration. Chapter 13 considers in greater detail the values necessary to support a politically inclusive climate majority. The necessity of building communities of support and mutual understanding receives further treatment in chapter 3. Here we will briefly suggest that all such work may require a basic foundation of *tolerance*.

It's true that to 'tolerate' does not necessarily entail respecting or appreciating other people, but merely 'putting up with' them. As a social goal, tolerance is often regarded as inadequate.[11] However, in the current urgent context (and perhaps at any time) we may recognize its value as an on-ramp to urgent collaboration in an increasingly fragmented society. Tolerant behaviour is a far lower barrier to entry than deep understanding, empathy or acceptance. It does not require that anybody change their views as a condition of cooperation.

What is more, even if our ultimate aim is true respect, we can do worse than begin with a more achievable ambition of tolerant behaviour. Once we are cooperating towards a shared purpose together, we have the opportunity to experience each other as fully dimensional and human, building the familiarity that supplants pre-existing assumptions about the other and that can underpin deeper empathy. Tolerance is an invaluable route to empathy because it gets us to the table in the first place.

Some may find the invitation to include those to whom they attribute intolerant beliefs paradoxical. We must therefore distinguish between rejecting intolerant *behaviour* and excluding everyone whose views we *assume* to be intolerant on the basis of, for example, their political identity. One is a valuable guiding principle. The other is the antithesis of an inclusive movement.

As chapter 4 will discuss, some promising community climate initiatives are founded upon the kinds of action-first approach mentioned above – strengthening latent bonds of community through local sustainability and adaptation work, including foundational work to identify common values in a supportive environment. Whereas polarization is fuelled by a simulated digital reality – one designed to manufacture outrage at an unseen other – tangible, pragmatic climate action allows people to reconnect with each other in the real world. It reveals climate and society as interconnected and mutually regenerative. Far from being just a necessary compromise, then, inclusive climate action can help us understand that a sustainable future begins in our relationships with each other.

TOWARDS MASS MOBILIZATION

In the long term we can expect that the world is heading towards a social tipping point in climate awareness and engagement. That a climate movement of some kind will eventually involve a majority of people appears close to inevitable. As the weather continues to deteriorate, and as government failure to act becomes ever more conspicuous, a majority will be motivated to engage by a more immediate sense of threat. What's less clear is whether this will happen quickly enough to prevent catastrophic harm. In response, we have sketched the case for something like a Climate Majority Project: a means of supporting a climate-concerned majority of people to respond in meaningful, joined-up ways to the climate and ecological emergency, and a rallying point wherein people may begin to see their actions as connected within a larger whole. We do not intend to describe or plan in detail how this diverse, distributed mobilization will be realized. Any attempt to do so would be hubristic in the extreme, not to mention simply impossible. The directions it takes will be determined by countless people, and by their unique talents, needs and capacities. Chapter 3, however, introduces the organization's published 'theory of change': an evolving set of principles that we hope can foster the conditions for such a mobilization to arise.

NOTES

1 By moderate we mean *tactically* moderate *compared with recent radical groups*. Aims remain radically transformative.

2 For example, Retrofit Balsall Heath, an inspiring zero-carbon project in Birmingham, is working with community partners to retrofit homes and community spaces, who collaborate with the Climate Majority Project.

3 See, for example, George, S. (2021). Which UK cities are the new climate 'A-Listers' – and why? Edie Newsroom, 19 November (www. edie.net/which-uk-cities-are-the-new-climate-a-listers-and-why/).

4 See, for example, Kollewe, J. (2022). BlackRock's Larry Fink: climate policies are about profits, not being 'woke'. Guardian, 18 January (www.theguardian.com/environment/2022/jan/18/blackrock-larry-fi nk-climate-policies-profits-woke). See also www.ceres.org/policy and www.gcsleaders.com/.

5 With thanks to Jay Wilson.

6 Note the politically diverse signatories of the Climate Majority Project's founding statement at www.climatemajorityproject.com/general -letter.

7 Nagel, T. (1986). *The View From Nowhere*. Oxford University Press (https://philpapers.org/rec/NAGTVF).

8 See, for example, Lawson, A. (2022). *The Entangled Activist*, p. 128. Perspectiva.

9 Hawken, P. (2021). *Regeneration: Ending the Climate Crisis in One Generation*. Penguin.

10 Read, R. (2021). *Parents for a Future*. Boiler House Press.

11 See, for example, Das, K. (2020). Tolerance has a fatal flaw. This is the solution. CNN Opinion (https://edition.cnn.com/2020/06/11/opinio ns/tolerance-will-never-be-enough-das/index.html).

PART II

FOUNDATION

CHAPTER 3

The Climate Majority Project: a theory of change

Liam Kavanagh and Rupert Read

A climate majority is forming, by which we mean that a majority of citizens feel mounting concern about climate change and government inaction, with growing potential to become engaged and turn their energies towards mass climate action. For now, many of those who constitute this trend are unaware of just how large it is, but we believe that mainstream climate action will actually succeed when the millions of people who want it understand that they are part of a powerful group and work consciously together. Climate is so all-encompassing a crisis that a mainstream climate movement is bound to form eventually. The basic question underpinning this theory of change is, therefore:

> How can we catalyse the tip towards mainstream climate action and system change that is already underway?

We will propose four deeply interdependent strands of activity that can help us face our dire situation and turn towards determined collective action:

- a narrative shift towards truthfulness;
- cultures of awareness and resilience;
- pragmatic action; and
- shared understanding.

CLARIFICATIONS

As simple as possible; no simpler

Some readers may hope for an A to Z manual of how a climate majority can form and bring about serious climate action, complete with a detailed plan for every kind of person. We only wish this were possible. Instead we discuss what can be done to create *conditions* to support a coherent climate movement to arise and drive society-wide mobilization. Such a mobilization will necessarily be distributed, emergent and bottom-up, i.e. not strictly plannable. This theory of change follows the advice to 'make things as simple as possible, and no simpler', and it also tries to be as precise as possible, but not more precise.

We realize that XR's initial plan to get 3.5% of the population out on the street was so motivating and unifying because it gave a simple and clear plan for addressing the climate crisis. But, unfortunately, as XR veterans found out, simple and clear plans to solve complex problems have a way of being attractive but ultimately insufficient.[1] Complexity is another thing we must be able to accept.

A more effective climate movement will be formed by millions of people finding their own part to play. It will be as complex as any wartime mobilization; more so, in fact, because it will be less state-led. We recognize with relief and excitement that such a movement is underway and that it is rapidly growing, across all sectors, at all levels and in most parts of the planet – not least because the weather calls for change more loudly every year. We are all on a journey into the unknown, encountering dangers – and maybe opportunities – on an unprecedented scale.

Which climate majority?

The Climate Majority Project is based in the UK but is globally aware. We work to catalyse the growth of a majority for climate action in the UK that is conscious of being just one part of the global active majority that serious climate action requires. A citizen majority in the UK is already climate-concerned – this project aims to create and strengthen channels for its activation.

We do not assume that this climate-concerned majority is homo-
geneous in its other views, needs or circumstances; and we are not
proposing a neat, 'one size fits all' climate movement that is somehow
definitively 'mainstream'. Rather, a core principle of the project is
supporting people to find the piece of climate action that is relevant
to themselves within a myriad of initiatives: those that already exist
and those yet to be born, specific to people and place.

We cannot speak on behalf of the movement that is forming. We
speak for ourselves, while offering analysis and vision that we hope
will prove valuable to others.

THE DYNAMICS OF INACTION: WHAT EXACTLY ARE WE UP AGAINST?

While established institutions have shown that they cannot mount a
sane and effective response to the climate and ecological emergency
(CEE), still they manage to preserve their own sense of authority
and necessity. Amid radical uncertainty we can nonetheless say with
confidence that no established political or industrial player has the
will or the power, within the established rules, to ensure the changes
necessary to limit overheating to 1.5°C or even 2°C. Very few call for
sufficiently deep changes to the systems and rules of society. Such
changes to the established order would threaten that order itself –
our current systems of government and economics – as well as the
lifestyles of many voters. An insider of the political or industrial elite
who proposes such changes will have great difficulty remaining on
the inside. So, though many insiders do what they can about the
climate crisis, without jeopardizing either their position or the institution they represent, it is not nearly enough.

A critical example is the interaction of institutional politics and
science to downplay the severity of human-caused climate change.
For example, the IPCC process demonstrates bias towards mini-
mizing the crisis, offering long-delayed recognition of dangerous
'non-linearities' in the climate system while quickly and uncritically
embracing 'solutions' like carbon capture technology. Some scientific, sociological and political voices do constructively criticize the
IPCC, but concerns about jeopardizing the IPCC process mean that,

typically, even critics participate in an institutional dynamic that in effect asks us to remain excessively calm while failing to produce the urgent action that both institutions and critics admit is necessary.

The same instinct shows up in scientists' and politicians' claims that 'staying below 1.5°C is still possible', while the meaning of 'possible' remains ambiguous. That is, meeting 1.5 is 'technically' or 'physically' possible, but realizing this possibility would require an abrupt and deep change in our politics in the very near future – a change that there are few signs of. Established institutions have no way of addressing the problem and do not want to say so, for fear of provoking a crisis of confidence. But preserving this dynamic is extremely unwise: democracy cannot respond appropriately to a situation if its severity is not publicly understood.

Our purpose in laying out the grim tale above is not to cast institutional insiders as 'the bad guys' or critics as failures. What we are asserting is that widespread intellectual agreement with the idea of a climate crisis is not translating into action because of subtle ways in which we and our institutions unwittingly cooperate to persuade each other that everything is OK. We ask readers to reflect on the potential of more deeply felt public awareness to dispel complacency and open new fields of possibility for action.

A new window of opportunity

The good news is that a lot of people have noticed the inability of our governments and economic systems to appropriately address the climate and other societal crises. They have been talking about it – a lot – and coming up with their own responses. As this trend grows it can lead to a 'non-linearity' in the human social system: similar to those seen in the climate system, but vastly more welcome. Deep social change was scoffed at thirty years ago when dangerous climate change first became mainstream news, but it is increasingly viewed as possible and desirable – even inevitable. The word 'polycrisis' – a term that encapsulates the current set of ecological breakdowns, economic turmoil, information breakdowns and institutional distrust and that signals the need for a major change in the global order – has become a 'new global buzzword',[2] appearing in mainstream publications such as the *Financial Times*,[3] in the communications of EU and UN agencies[4] and civil society organizations,[5] and as the theme of the World Economic Forum's 2023 meeting in Davos.[6]

Opportunities arise as people realize that business-as-usual, politics-as-usual and thinking-as-usual have hit a wall, and seek new voices articulating new routes to a sane future. Scouring podcasts for non-mainstream views is itself now a mainstream activity. The great pace of technological innovation is increasingly matched by voices questioning the assumption that technology alone can solve our crises. Even conservative audiences have begun to question the doctrine that market forces can, on their own, deliver green lifestyles at scale.[7] Understanding that widespread popular cooperation to halt global overheating is needed will, in this environment, become more and more like common sense. At the same time, many are starting to realize that life might be better if it were simpler, if communities were stronger and if incomes were more stable and secure.

WHAT MIGHT WE DO ABOUT IT?

We intend to help catalyse the mainstream climate movement that is underway and whose growth is inevitable. A movement is forming of people drawn from, and speaking to, many walks of life. They are working at both institutional and popular levels, finding common cause and getting started on doing what clearly needs to be done, while working to create agreement on more contentious steps. Deteriorating weather and continuing inaction will drive recognition that waiting for institutions and 'leaders' to address the situation is futile, and more people will get on with the task at hand.

The emergent movement needs to be large and creative, and it *will* be, because the worsening climate situation is pushing us towards a social tipping point in climate awareness and action. Everybody, including the rich and powerful, will be worse off after a catastrophe – a fact that is ever more widely recognized. The next big thing will not be just one thing: it will be *lots* of things, broadly aligned. It will comprise many people finding their own way to contribute, networked with others. The question is: will it be fast enough? The Climate Majority Project exists to humbly do our best to ensure the answer to that question is yes.

The public we seek to bring together is diverse, with diverse circumstances, opportunities and capacities, and those involved are at different stages on their own 'climate journey', from newly concerned to fully engaged. Accordingly, our theory of change is not linear – X leading to Y leading to Z. Rather, we see interdependent 'strands' of a rope: none sufficient by itself, but strong enough *together* to pull enormous weight.

Four strands of change for a climate majority

Narrative shift

Shifting climate conversations further towards truthfulness, regarding both the depth of the challenges faced and the emerging responses. Fostering the motivation and understanding needed to break inertia.

Collective resilience

Cultivating the community and resources that can underpin mutual support through inevitably difficult experiences and emotions, and the belonging, co-concern and shared endeavour that can take us from despair to determination.

Tangible actions

Supporting citizens to find   pragmatic and well-thought-out ways to make specific changes together, turning concern into meaningful climate action.

Building shared understanding

Promoting an ongoing, inclusive, agenda-setting conversation lays the groundwork for tomorrow's tangible actions, and surveys the shifting social landscape. In particular, people involved in mainstream climate action need shared understanding of how their personal (local) actions play a role in global efforts by millions – giving individuals confidence that their efforts are not wasted.

These four strands weave together to create the confident main-stream action we sorely need. They are how we help each other cope, build resilience in our communities, and become deeply moti-vated to energetically undertake co-created potent responses to the climate emergency.

The discussion that follows outlines each strand; their impor-tance to a popular, emergent, widely credible climate mobilization; and the particular actions that the Climate Majority Project intends to take. In undertaking this discussion, we remain deeply aware that the expression of these strands will vary among subcultures and sec-tors of economic activity. The complexity the coming climate move-ment must encompass is just one more reason why we are so wary of proposing any theory of change that might sound simple and neat.

Strand 1: a narrative shift towards truthfulness

A motivated climate majority requires effective communication about the gravity of the climate emergency. For millions of people to make effective plans together, truthful communication is required – not 'elite' figures telling people what they need to hear. The truth-fulness we need includes naming institutional barriers to addressing climate change.

All those who know it need to speak this truth clearly: we must let go of the belief that there is still time to 'fix the climate'. All is not lost, and every fraction of a degree of warming we can now prevent is critically important, but some precious things are already lost and some targets are no longer attainable. Denial of these facts props up trust that institutions can still deliver safety, when they have already failed. For years and years we have been told that it is 'five minutes to midnight' – in reality, the clock has continued to move.

Inevitably, many would rather not hear, or dwell on, this alarming new story. Nonetheless, many already *sense* it at some level. Most of us know the truth, at the fringes of our awareness – in nagging anxiety that rises with each regular report of freakish weather. Each person who breaks the hegemonic social silence on accepting climate chaos makes it easier for others to bring it out into the open. It makes the illusion that business-as-usual can go on harder and harder to maintain.

This truth is easier to tell now that the IPCC all but admits that 'climate-safety' – the hospitable climate of our ancestors – is now behind us. The idea that '1.5 is still alive' depends on technology that has yet to be invented.[8] Politically, it depends on abrupt action by the same old institutions. We are at the very brink of 1.5 now, because we failed to make reductions long ago when they were clearly needed. There are not even plans in place to rectify this clear failure, let alone a process that seems capable of delivering them. James Hansen, the former director of NASA who first emphasized the climate threat to US policymakers, has declared that 'there is no chance whatever' of staying below 1.5°C, and more and more experts[9] now publicly urge acceptance that the Paris Agreement has failed in its objective of keeping us safe from dangerous climate change. We agree.

Climate effects that are now inevitable in 'frontline' states in the Global South are finessed with soft-denialist pretences that 1.5°C is still possible, while the dire need for adaptation – let alone seriously accounting for 'loss and damage' – is denied and delayed. There will never be adequate funding for transformative adaptation so long as populations are complacently assured that 'there is still time' to limit warming to a 'safe' 1.5°C. The rigorous truthfulness of this first strand is therefore essential to achieving any kind of climate justice.

It is also untruthful, and dangerously hubristic, to suggest that rich societies in the Global North are immune from climate consequences. This attitude is found among some climate justice activists, and it is rarely considered that we too – especially, perhaps, the poorest among us – might turn out to be on 'the climate frontline'. In the dawning age of endemic climate-related disasters, the Covid emergency should have been a warning shot, starkly revealing the fragility of (poorly governed) 'developed' countries, while poorer countries in, for example, West Africa and East Asia proved relatively robust. Countries such as the UK that depend heavily on long supply chains can expect, for example, to feel heavily the coming disruptions in world food production.

We seek a shift in understanding of human-caused climate change away from abstract, distant and slow physical impacts (sea level rise, glacier melt, etc.) and towards nearer-term and locally understood effects (food security, pandemics, mass migrations, etc.). The climate crisis will not be a spectator sport.

A line in the sand

Though we are almost certain to cross a danger line (1.5°) that our institutions drew themselves, scientific communities and most political 'leaders' remain generally reluctant to level with the general public. The decision to maintain optimism by softening facts represents a gamble vastly at odds with how the public manages and outsources other risks in everyday life.

Public Health England, for example, recommends that we live a healthy life. It does not sanction getting drunk and eating junk food every day on the optimistic expectation that by 2050 our ruined health will be restored by a speculative wonder pill. Nobody wants to live in buildings or fly in planes built by 'optimistic' engineers or architects, but we are building the future of our planet around wildly optimistic assumptions. This ill-advised gamble is not explicitly acknowledged. We believe that it must be.

That the scientific establishment avoids telling disturbing truths in this area is clearly evidenced, for example, by the IPCC's belated admission of dangerous feedback cycles, its temporary acceptance of 2.0°C as an acceptable risk on political rather than scientific grounds, and its willingness to rely on speculative tech in forecasting carbon reductions. Meanwhile, some of science's top climate communicators issue repeated statements that the public must at all costs not be panicked.[10]

We believe institutional insiders – including scientific and political leadership – should treat the public like adults and level with us about what they really think. Trusted figures who openly express awareness of institutional failure should not appear as pessimistic 'outliers' but as they are: a minority brave enough to say out loud what the majority thinks.

Truth and agency: a generative interaction

Some prominent voices in the climate space resist this level of realism, on the basis that it leads to doomism and inaction. However, we should note that when Greta Thunberg said 'I want you to panic' and 'the house is on fire', her statements helped to catapult her and the school strike movement to international fame and admiration. Furthermore, among many theories about why XR has not achieved its goals, none suggest that the movement was simply too truthful. The ongoing emergence of citizen climate action (strand 3) also testifies to public robustness in the face of truth. Our experience in speaking to hundreds of people suggests that, on balance, a suspicion that things are worse than governments admit on climate – and that governments' responses have been inadequate – does not lead citizens to curl up in despair but rather to ask themselves what they can do. As their positive actions become visible to others, the basis for a truthful societal narrative likewise grows stronger.

The truth about top-down change: the role of a revitalized electorate

The truthful messaging we advocate includes honesty about the state of public support for serious climate action at policy level, and the challenges we face in growing it. The unrealistic idea that a few of us can force authorities to 'just change' has underwritten many climate campaigns, over a long period. *More* voters with *enough* concern to make hard choices are still required to force politicians to face the difficulties of climate action or be replaced.

This statement may be surprising, given recent shifts in public climate awareness. We stress that while popular awareness has increased, it still has a long way to go. Polls show that there is already a climate majority – but our resolve badly needs deepening. A majority of people report concern about climate and nature, especially after extreme weather such as record heatwaves and droughts in the UK. Polls in 2022 found that 32% of the population said they were 'very worried' and a further 44% said they were 'somewhat worried' about man-made climate change. But are those people concerned enough to undertake the difficulties of climate action? Encouragingly, about two-thirds of voters support tax rises to pay for carbon mitigation, and a majority support a tax that would make CO_2-producing products pricier. But another poll in 2021, *before* the cost-of-living crisis kicked in, asked more specific questions and got less encouraging answers. Most respondents did not support increasing the cost of gas, petrol or meat. Politicians are understandably hesitant to take responsibility for ambitious policies when the public supports these in the abstract but objects to feeling their effects.

The public's seeming inconsistency is quite understandable. A major concern is whether raising prices for fossil fuels in the UK would *really* help lower world CO_2 emissions. After all, there is no guarantee that the rest of the world will do the same. A display of leadership is all that anybody can *promise* that a UK-only clean transition would produce in the short term. There is good reason to suspect that other nations would join us, but advocates for climate action will not inspire confidence by trying to pass swiftly over concerns that costly national heroics could be internationally ignored.

An alliance of climate-concerned citizens must overcome significant political obstacles. Both ideological aversion to government intervention in markets and the cost of carbon mitigation present hurdles. Achieving zero emissions will require strong new regulations that many in the business community fear will normalize stronger interventions in industry affairs. Climate action inherently threatens the ideology that, left to themselves, markets inevitably produce the best result. Public support for this ideology has been crumbling since 2008, and many business leaders also see its limits, but its proponents are well organized and well funded, and it therefore has a strong presence in the media. Voters can overpower it, but public support must be high enough to overcome inevitable pushback.

Though it is fashionable to say that transition to a low-carbon economy is now possible because 'clean tech is better/cheaper', a rapid transition to renewables will still require policy support and it will be expensive (though well worth it). Furthermore, a reduction in energy demand – which many argue, compellingly, is essential to enable sustainability – will require substantive lifestyle changes. Just because electric cars are competitive with fossil-burning cars now does not mean that replacing existing cars (that often *could* continue to run for many thousands of miles) will not be costly. This is exactly the position of a power company that has an old fossil-burning power plant but would like to replace it with a renewable power source. 'Throwing out' the old plant that it already paid for and was planning to use for a decade or more and replacing it with a new plant means significant unplanned spending for the same benefit.

The cost of a quick switch to clean power plants will have to be paid by *somebody*. While, with the right policy steps, we *could* avoid shifting costs to citizens, scepticism is understandable. We are not saying that power plants should not be replaced; rather, that a rapid switch to a renewable UK grid will not necessarily come without extra cost for most citizens. At some level people know this, which is why simple claims that we should 'go renewable now, because renewables are cheaper' may not build trust in climate campaigners.

In short, in order to change our political class we need a reinvigorated electorate. Our theory of change accepts this need and looks to create the conditions for political renewal.

Thus far in regard to public attitudes we have highlighted only the comparatively easy aspect of necessary transformation: a transition to renewable energy. The full picture is considerably more complex and challenging: if carbon emissions are eliminated, but our economic system is otherwise left to run exactly as it has, our economy would still do such damage to the web of life (biodiversity) that ecological collapse would soon be upon us.

Realistically, we do not expect large-scale agreement in the near term about how our whole way of life must change. But it is time to discuss openly the cracks that we have all seen forming in society's foundations. Our first strand, then, is about cutting to the chase, and overcoming the temptation, still widespread, towards soft denial. This is the necessary first step towards agreement on the bold action we need to take.

A change to clear, truthful messaging will not of itself lead to a sea change in climate action. As already mentioned, a truthful narrative shift forms one key strand of a rope. The next strand helps us to *handle* the truth.

Strand 2: communities of awareness and resilience

In a time of unprecedented turbulence, a climate majority that engages with the truth will need sufficient inner skills and support to navigate difficult experiences and strong emotions.

While much climate action focuses on solutions to material problems, it serves neither our cause nor our resilience to treat psychological and emotional factors as if they were not part of the real world. Read any account of successful politics in adversity, and you will sense, for example, the necessity for community support, an ability to speak the truth both powerfully and without hatred, and skill for shared self-care. Figures such as Gandhi, Nelson Mandela and Martin Luther King Jr are just a few well-known examples. It is strange that while these leaders are feted, and the centrality of their inner capacities to their accomplishments is so well known, no lesson is *commonly* drawn that successful transformative social movements must support psychological resources. We aspire to change that.

Whether considering collaboration and change at a mass level or facing difficult choices and painful climate consequences as a society, understanding and support of inner capacities are crucial considerations at all levels of a movement. And in a space of uncertainty and rapid change, where responsibility weighs heavy and plans are prone to falling apart, organizers have a particular need for inner stability and shared practices for grounding and resilience-building. Whereas emotional dependence on particular stances, plans and strategies breeds resistance to change, the stability we find in community and strong internal resources will allow us to adjust our perspectives and strategies as often and as deeply as we will need to.

Supporting truth-hearing to become truth-knowing
The Climate Majority Project will not succeed in raising much-needed awareness by brow-beating those who deny dangerous human-caused climate change or its implications and ambushing them with the truth. Really listening to truth entails accepting existential threat and personal responsibility within a complex, unsustainable system, and dealing with significant anxiety. We must therefore organize to genuinely support each other in facing a common threat and counteracting feelings of isolation and helplessness. People who are suddenly hit by the gravity of what we are facing benefit from talking to others like them, especially those who have felt the same emotions before. People who are 'swimming against the current' in their workplace or community benefit from knowing others who are doing the same.

In fact, the word 'denial' itself, with its negative associations, may not even serve us well. It is entirely human to find more optimistic versions of the facts appealing. Most of us experience some urge to subtly reframe facts to make climate breakdown less threatening, and to exaggerate our own ability to 'solve' it. Like the belief that future technology will save the day, the view that existing political processes (such as the COP systems) will suddenly deliver big policy shifts is entirely understandable. It is a laborious process to separate the versions of the facts that withstand scrutiny from the versions that simply feel good, but doing so is a vital task for the climate majority. It is best undertaken with the help of others who listen closely and raise objections carefully and with empathy. As per twelve-step programmes, grief counselling and support groups, accepting the situation and its depth can be the first step to dealing with it, but acceptance is itself a process that cannot be short circuited.

The opportunity to speak one's mind and be heard by supportive others is widely understood to be helpful in accepting virtually any difficult situation, whether that is an unwelcome medical diagnosis, an addiction or a neighbourhood tragedy. A large number of initiatives already provide a space to feel into and to face the fears that come with contemplating environmental catastrophe (see chapter 13).

The public health crisis of climate anxiety may present an opportunity to advance this conversation. Three-quarters of the UK population is worried about the climate, with 32% being 'very worried' and 5% worried enough for their day-to-day functioning to be impaired.[11] This 5% figure rose to 28% among a study focused on young people.[12] In particular, today's youth know they will be dealing with the age of consequences in what should have been their best years. Their anxiety is perfectly rational.

Our first action under this strand is to work with both the therapeutic community and community groups focused on climate, linking them together with media-savvy advocates (therapists are not particularly well positioned to be their own advertisers) to help such work grow its profile.

Conversations about shared resilience require the utmost care, because mental health concerns are traditionally marginalized, as are valuable practices (like mindfulness) that can be (wrongly) perceived as elitist, coercive, distracting or 'woo-woo'. Discussion of psychological resilience can become a barrier if it takes place in an inaccessible vocabulary – and we must respect that such resilience is highly personal and there is not one correct way to approach it. The Climate Majority Project must speak publicly about the core aspects of the inner challenge clearly and accessibly, while understanding that communities of support will use a variety of vocabularies suited to their members' own culture and practices.

Key aspects of strand 2 receive extended treatment in chapter 13.

Strand 3: tangible pragmatic actions

A large and growing number of newly climate-concerned citizens has the will and capacity to make a difference in how institutions operate, through well-chosen, practical channels appropriate to their own circumstances.

The most common question we encounter when talking to concerned citizens is: 'What can I *do?*' There are as many answers as there are people asking. The concerned climate majority has the potential to become a mass mobilization of citizens in diverse, distributed, mostly self-organizing action for climate mitigation, adaptation and protection of nature, combining to drive change at every institutional level and on all timescales. Our own task is not only to support and motivate this shift but also, crucially, to communicate a sense of the movement's aggregate leverage, empowering participants and showing decisionmakers its true size and reach (see strand 4).

We do not suggest that we will be responsible for this mainstream climate action. The kind of citizen initiatives we describe are already emerging and will continue to arise spontaneously as climate disruption impinges ever further on daily life – but the pace can be increased.

The catch-22 of climate (in)action
Addressing climate and ecological breakdown requires something like a war effort, allowing individuals to participate in something far bigger than themselves. Needless to say, this has not yet happened, and it will not do so until governments are forced to draw up these plans by citizens. However, people must more fully accept the situation before they can effectively confront the government – but many do not want to think about it because they feel too small and

isolated to do anything about it. There is no sense of effective coordination, which is usually the government's job. This is the catch-22 of climate (in)action.

A coordinated citizen response

What we need in the near term, then, is a coordinated response that starts *without* the government. People doing whatever can be done without policy support. The Climate Majority Project invites everyone to organize, wherever in life they have most agency, power or leverage. This may be within extended families, neighbourhoods, workplaces, professions or elsewhere.

In some cases, the right organizations already exist. In the workplace, for example, we may look to sector-specific groups such as Lawyers for Net Zero (for corporate lawyers) and certain Trade Unions. Where the right, capable, salient organization already exists, the task is straightforward: join and actively support it. In most other cases, the task is to self-organize.

The form this work takes will be determined by its many participants. All can benefit from finding others who share their fears and intentions. Many will need to take a journey of *finding the work that is theirs to do*, along with others.

Climate agency through vigorous pragmatism

As the philosopher Roberto Unger notes, political debate tends to swing between 'practical' but uninspiring marginal changes and inspiring but impractical utopian visions.[13] The work we propose charts a middle path.

In contrast to the radical climate movement, the Climate Majority Project will not concentrate, in the near term, on demanding that national or international governmental institutions make the deepest required changes (macro level). Instead we encourage taking the boldest and most important steps that are possible *now* and that will make more steps possible later. In practice, this means thousands of people creating change *at the highest institutional level they can*. This could mean changes in communities, workplaces, faith groups, universities and targeted aspects of national government 'today' and sweeping changes in national governments' policies 'tomorrow'. It can also include policies amenable to today's politics that would allow a climate majority to form more quickly. Our attitude of realism accepts that major macro changes are unlikely in the short term via current methods but that we may build towards them via tangible successes at different institutional levels. This really is a marathon, not a sprint. Or better, it is a relay race: some people must do the running today so that others can do it tomorrow.

Similarly, realism forbids focusing on individual changes in consumer behaviour. Sufficient change by individuals, unsupported by institutions and collective campaigns, is extremely unlikely. Furthermore, a key barrier to entry into active change-making is a (justified) sense that what one does alone will not be very meaningful.

Initially, then, the Climate Majority Project will effect change through intermediate institutional action, operating within core arenas of *collective* agency – particularly, but *not* limited to, workplaces (including businesses and professions) and geographic communities. The constituency participating in this action will both take direct responsibility for leading and implementing practical change and use tangible successes, influence and organization to generate more collective agency and enable action at higher levels. All of this will, in turn, contribute to change in the political culture at large.

Citizen action in workplaces and communities is a central pillar of the Climate Majority Project, and as such it receives extended treatment in chapter 4.

Geographic communities

Activity in geographic communities will tend towards local initiatives for adaptation, resilience and improvements in quality of living (which is not at all the same thing as expanded material consumption). Adaptation has received little attention in mainstream consideration of climate response because it breaks the taboo against accepting the reality of climate chaos. Emphasis on adaptation and preparedness can powerfully shift consciousness by connecting us with our vulnerability in ways that strategies for 'fixing' climate decline do not. After all, if we are *adapting* to something, then it is obviously real – and important. Because this shift in consciousness can catalyse all kinds of further climate action, adaptation for resilience will take high priority for the Climate Majority Project.

For many, *community climate action* will be a natural way to embody leadership, especially because engagement in forms of transformative adaptation and resilience building has the potential to activate many other people. As a first-rate example, the Climate Majority Project incubator is supporting Community Climate Action, an organization offering citizens routes to highly tangible, meaningful action. Scaled up, such organizations have extraordinary transformative potential. (Community Climate Action is discussed further in chapter 5.)

The workplace

Compared with civil society and the political realm, the professions and labour generally remain quiet on climate and nature. Most people still spend half of their waking weekday hours at work (even if, for many of us, work now takes place at home). An enormous portion of our power is exercised in this context. Climate Majority Project efforts will direct some of that time and energy towards employee-driven change from within relevant organizations.

Workplaces offer wide possibilities for change: from sustainable adaptation and location of premises, to the decarbonizing of supply chains, to the nature of products and pension funds. As we explore in chapters 4 and 11, some areas of employment represent particularly crucial pinch points in the system: these include, for example, law, pension-fund management, insurance, audit and transport. Shifts in priorities and operations within these areas can precipitate rapid progress across other sectors, and the Climate Majority Project focuses support on areas of highest leverage.

Harnessing the massive lobbying and brand power of business is ever more realistic as the foundations of business become increasingly vulnerable to climate impacts. Concerned businesses can draw down their emissions significantly within existing rules, but they must also lobby for new rules that would force all emissions to zero – both their own and those of competitors: levelling the playing field is necessary to avoid a race to the bottom. For business (including finance) to call for its own better and more stringent regulation in the interest of self-preservation, rather than asking for regulatory exemptions, would be a newsworthy 'man bites dog' moment. Employees can have real influence in national policy by turning their employer into a lobbyist for new, sane market rules.

Encouraging signs

Some businesses are already demonstrating strong moral leadership on climate. In 2022 Patagonia founder Yvon Chouinard gave the company away to a trust that will divert all profits into fighting the environmental crisis, using the wealth the company creates 'to protect the source of all wealth'.[14]

Our own experience in presenting a five-past-midnight narrative to open-minded businesspeople upholds the proposition that narrative shift, communities of resilience and pragmatic action support one another. Within a sufficiently supportive environment, once business leaders have the opportunity to understand the depth of the problem, the impossibility of sufficient quick wins, their organizations' vulnerability and the failure of government 'leadership', minds and hearts often open towards meaningful action. Conversely, the visibility of pragmatic options makes it easier to accept and operate within a new narrative. Serious contemplation of climate action starts when both awareness of the issue and the possibility of effective response come to the fore. Most are relieved to hear that there is a way forward that does not involve glueing themselves to the M25 (which they are unwilling to do). As we explain in our discussion of strand 4 below, what many businesses still need is a sense that their action will truly be part of something large enough to matter, and therefore worth undertaking.

Moderate 'direct' action and potential for escalation

We prioritize the reasonable, legal actions of citizens, in their own initiatives, for practical climate action. If and when these reasonable asks and actions are resisted, however, the potential exists to ratchet up collective action. For instance, transformative adaptation initiatives that meet government resistance may consider escalating to non-violent direct action to enable their goals. Wild Card is another Climate Majority Project incubatee that seeks to drive rewilding of the Crown Estates. The Duchies, having resisted its reasonable ask, might experience some guerrilla rewilding. Resistance to change in workplaces may occasion climate strikes. And if businesses seeking policy change meet resistance from government, then they may consider previously unused tactics such as withholding a percentage of owed tax.

Imitation and translation

Those seeking to organize have much to learn from approaches that have seen success elsewhere. We can look to extant transformative adaptation endeavours in Nepal or Rojava, for example; to remarkable non-profits such as Bosch; to the resilience of Cuba from 1991 onwards under incredible 'peak oil' pressure; to the outstanding carbon reduction achievements of Denmark (made possible, in part, by wide community 'buy-in' to renewable energy, as well as by policy innovations in this field and others at the state level); or to the outrider success of countries such as Bhutan and New Zealand on moving beyond obsession with economic growth.

It is also necessary to popularize good practices from within the 'progressive bubble'. For example, the Transition Town Movement has done great things in dozens of countries, but it mostly succeeds in towns with large 'progressive' populations. Work to address eco-anxiety or reconnect with nature demonstrates similar patterns. These ideas can in principle have broad appeal, but in practice any organization's culture tends to reflect the background of its membership. Many existing progressive initiatives therefore need help translating their learnings to be accessible to new populations.

The Climate Majority Project incubator

Much of our energy is concentrated on providing funding and expertise to people acting on good new ideas to get climate action into the mainstream. The Climate Majority Project incubator gathers funding from concerned investors and supports social entrepreneurs with financial, strategic, psychological and networking input. We are working with partners to help expand the services that we can assist nascent climate majority groups with, including a social media and web presence, tech advice, legal advice and so on.

The idea is taken from business, where incubators provide the expertise and skills that all new businesses need. At the moment we consider climate majority work similar to the early days of online business, when a number of good new ideas had been advanced to a great stage of readiness and simply needed funding from a first wave of incubators/investors in order to become viable. As internet retail drew attention, and the money drawn towards online business increased, the next wave of incubators became more full-service affairs, starting to help entrepreneurs at earlier and earlier stages of development. This was typically done by drawing in people who had acted as CEO in the first wave of business. Analogously, we are funding individuals and small groups (some of them already quite experienced in business or campaigning) who can act as advisors to the next wave of climate majority enterprises, who we expect will be supported by a growing wave of willing funders.

Strand 4: building shared understanding

Finally, the emerging climate majority requires a process for making wider sense of the world and informing collective action, and for deepening the kinds of 'big picture' considerations outlined above. As already mentioned, we dispute the possibility of up-front, comprehensive plans for building mainstream, serious climate action. Instead we believe that a credible and democratic process for shared understanding must patiently be built with allies from across the political spectrum. Such a process must both name long-term ambitious goals and continually plan a series of next steps on the journey towards those goals.

This process will bring diverse groups aligned with the Climate Majority Project together in an embodiment of intelligent democracy. Importantly, it can give many people a chance to see their actions as part of a larger whole, potent enough to matter.

An effort for transition that creates such a sense of shared endeavour will emerge from a community that shares deep intentions and is constantly growing and diversifying while deepening bonds of trust and solidarity. We can more easily trust people, communities and processes to guide us than we can trust plans for transition created by people we do not know through a process we are not part of. So, even if a small group of planners were to create a plan with sufficient detail to actually be a blueprint for transition, they would have little success convincing the population of that plan's merits. For comparison, remember the climate science community's difficulty in convincing people of well-founded, but inherently complex, arguments. Planning to build trust is then the paramount challenge of planning.

Trust can be built by working together, and our first three strands of action provide the conditions that will allow more people to work together as part of a credible transition process. At the moment it is impossible to have a sufficiently democratic conversation about systems change because awareness of the depth of transition necessary is still concentrated among a narrow set of people. There can be no motivation if we do not know what is at stake and if a unifying conversation is not happening. But the goals of truthfulness in communicating our predicament (strand 1); increased emotional support (strand 2); and finding actions that can appeal to, and usefully absorb the energies of, the broadest segments of climate-concerned citizens (strand 3) allow a community to form around urgent climate action. Within these communities of trust and collaboration, the conversation can deepen.

Challenges and formative principles of the shared understanding process

As already mentioned, the process of developing shared understanding involves deciding on next steps while keeping in mind and preparing for long-term challenges. Here we briefly lay out some key near-term sense-making challenges facing the climate majority and a set of principles that will inform our long-term process for building shared understanding.

Key near-term challenges

Making the climate majority aware of itself. A foundational sense-making task, and luckily one of the easier ones, is to help people become aware of the emergence and growth of the climate majority itself.

For people thinking of organizing in their community, workplace, extended family or faith group, it is incredibly helpful to see that others near and far are doing the same thing: waking up, organizing, looking for the others. The more that people are aware of the same kind of thing happening across many domains, the greater encouragement they feel, and the greater their willingness to put effort into an endeavour big enough that it *just might work*.

To get a feeling for the emotional importance of this task, consider the following example. Imagine a young person tells her friends and family that she wants to work to respond to climate decline. Her family's responses may often land somewhere between playful teasing and mockery: 'So, you want to save the world?' If the same person said 'I want to organize the world's information', the response might be similar, but if she said the same thing after being hired by Google, the reaction will change. Her family might approve or disapprove, but they would have no grounds on which to mock. And yet, though many more people are part of climate action than work at Google, the climate movement's great size often fails to translate into the perception that its members' individual efforts are part of a potent collective endeavour. (In contrast, Google's cohesiveness makes its many employees' small actions seem like part of a potent larger plan.) Low cohesiveness among climate campaigners can make their individual actions feel meaningless, even if their goal is incredibly meaningful.

So, if people see their contribution as part of a far larger endeavour, the sense of agency dramatically increases. Further, willingness to be part of mainstream climate action is helped when we see that its emergence is inevitable. Its greatest recruiter, after all, is the weather, which will become more convincing every year.

Successful outreach across demographics. Building shared understanding requires learning how to spread climate awareness among different segments of the population. Our funded audience research work – advised by George Marshall (founder of Climate Outreach) and building on Britain Talks Climate[15] – is exploring this task. Whole books have been written on this subject; this short section of our book focuses on just a few key points.

First, a segment of the population that researchers call progressive activists – highly educated, mostly urban people, who think globally and who identify with political issues such as inequality and injustice – has traditionally dominated climate action, but a climate *majority* can only be convened by listening to other concerned segments and addressing their specific concerns. Many people think in more local terms than progressives, and are more interested in practical concerns than abstract ones.

For example, as mentioned in strand 3, talking about adaptation is helpful for reaching people who think locally. Though carbon levels in the atmosphere are a global phenomenon, their effects are local. Preparing for the effects of climate chaos is far more practical on a local than a global level, and adaptation is therefore arguably a very effective way of broaching the subject of climate to localists, who make up most of the electorate. It is impossible to prepare for local effects caused by climate without gaining climate awareness. This will in turn translate into a willingness to reduce emissions (as well as having a direct impact).

Among segments of the population that are openly patriotic and conservative, motivating ideas include, for example, 'defending what we hold dear' and 'showing leadership'.[16] Climate decline is a threat to the national interest, and many patriotic people are more motivated to defend their country from the effects of climate breakdown than they are by calls to altruism on behalf of the most affected countries. While most people have elements of both of these concerns, self-interested impulses are less often expressed publicly.

Similarly, the chance to show some genuine world leadership on climate and biodiversity/conservation has the potential to appeal to conservatives. It will be a great boost to global climate action if a country such as the UK starts moving towards net zero ambitiously, wherever the motivation comes from. The world might benefit from a country being willing to 'go it alone' to some extent on climate, so Britain's independent and even patriotic streak has potential advantages.

Navigating divisive questions. A number of questions can cause division among people who see the need for climate action. While we do

not have to come to final answers, polarizing questions must be identified and given thought early and often. For example, if we ignore
questions such as those surrounding 'green growth' early, they will
be more divisive later on.

Formative principles

*Rapidly reducing net carbon emissions to near zero is necessary, and it
is only likely to come about as part of a deep effort for systems change.*
What exactly this systems change looks like, and what other long-
term goals must necessarily accompany zero emissions, will become
clearer gradually, and patience is needed for this consensus to form
and broaden.

*Carbon neutrality cannot be achieved while leaving the rest of our sys-
tem intact, because our system is itself unsustainable in various ways.*
Biodiversity is an obvious example: simply replacing fossil fuel technology with green technology will not stop the ongoing extinctions
of hundred of thousands of species – and, as our best scientists warn
us, we humans will directly feel the effects of our assaults on the
web of life soon.[17] As the physicist Thomas Murphy says: 'If squirrels
could speak, they'd be rooting for us to fail to transition to green
energy, because humans' access to massive amounts of energy has
always been used to destroy and exploit natural systems.'

*Climate action must explore synergy with wider systems change on many
levels.* Many aspects of human systems invite change: our basic priorities, our political polarization, our market-centric ideology, our
wise use of technology and artificial intelligence, our colonialism,
our corporate unaccountability, and so on. Climate breakdown can
be seen as one potentially fatal symptom of the deeply unhealthy
habits of our economic and political systems, which are out of
touch with the needs of thriving life. Though we see the need for
system change, we focus on the climate and ecological crisis because,
at least for the people of the UK, climate is the clearest and most
widely agreed upon threat to its own existence that our broken system has created. Failure to address climate chaos can more clearly

demonstrate the brokenness of our system, for more people, than any other social issue.

Shared understanding will build solidarity with the rest of the world. The nature of climate as a universal systemic issue entails that acting out of self-interest can become an accessible *route* to global solidarity. Radical climate activism often prescribes a stance of global justice and solidarity that, while admirable, can have the effect of alienating segments of the population whose concerns rest closer to home. Even when they become engaged out of localized concerns, however, citizens of the Global North will be in a position to see that humanity's prevailing economic systems threaten life on earth and that we have potential allies far and wide who face similar threats. Once we better understand how broken systems created the common threat of climate breakdown, we will more easily understand, and sympathize with, the wider implications of those systems for other people in other places – people who are exposed to the most brutal aspects of world economic systems. Therefore, climate is a great place to start in an effort towards systems change, though it is not the only place to start and it is not the place to stop.

We need pragmatism, not defeatism or utopianism, on climate justice. The climate justice conversation, for all of its good intent, risks becoming utopian in character: seeking a way to right all of the world's wrongs in record time, to arrive at total global justice. This would certainly be desirable, but the job of the pragmatist is to practise the art of the possible. Finding the best course possible does not mean letting go of ideals, but instead seeing them as a compass in a political landscape filled with hills, gaps and seas. We seek others who favour a political identity built around deeply concerned pragmatism – and around a shared *process*, a lived 'thrutopia'[18] or 'protopia'[19] – rather than any fixed ideology.

We are over (material) growth. Prioritizing growth in material wealth gave our ancestors longer lives and access to many pleasures that were previously undreamed of, but we have long since passed the point at which national pursuit of growth is creating greater happiness for most people in the UK. Growth in fairness, in the health of natural environments, in community and free time are all more effective routes to better lives than growth in wealth. Fixation on economic growth is 'so last century'. It is time to move on to more important things. We see a need for a massive increase in creative experimentation and imagination with new ways of incentivizing economic behaviour that creates real value.

FOUR STRANDS INTERWEAVING

We offer a succinct summary of our four strands, and their essential interrelationship to form a 'rope' strong enough for our purpose.

(1) A narrative shift toward truthfulness.

(2) Communities of awareness and resilience.

(3) Tangible pragmatic actions.

(4) Building shared understanding.

   In short, facing the truth (1) can motivate action (3), and it is a condition for the right *kind* of action. Action in turn lends power to truth (1) and grows the constituency for mutual support (2). Communities of awareness, resilience and mutual support (2) help us hear, accept and *cope* with the truth (1). They nourish, incubate and empower our actions (3) and ease our process of shared understanding (4). Making sense of things together gives us the clarity we need to understand and speak the truth (1), to choose wise actions (3) and to identify our networks of mutual support (2).
   All four strands are essential. Each reinforces the others, and in fact they cannot entirely be distinguished from one another. It is their profound interaction that generates potential transformative scalability. Millions can be offered hope and faith by the energizing effect of remaining aware of the trouble, of finding meaningful routes to action, and of feeling like part of an emerging historical movement (a climate majority).

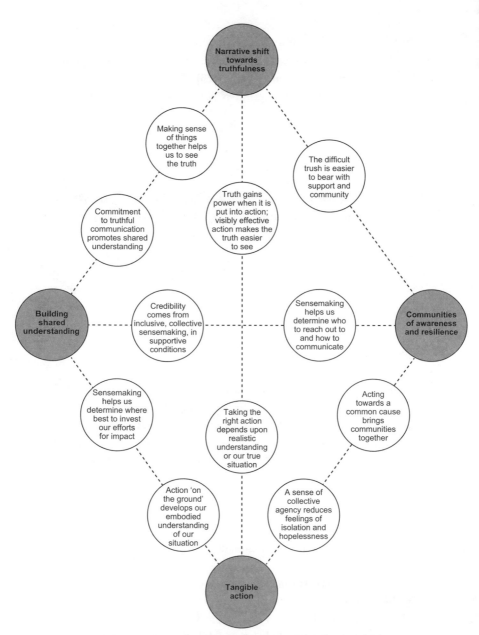

Figure 1. Four interdependent strands of activation.

NOTES

1 Paraphrasing H. L. Mencken.

2 See, for example, Goswami, M. (2023). The new global buzzword is polycrisis – what does it mean & should it worry you? *TheQuint*, 4 February.

3 Derbyshire, J. (2023). Year in a word: polycrisis. *Financial Times*, 1 January. See also Tooze, A. (2022). Welcome to the world of the polycrisis. *Financial Times*, 28 October.

4 See, for example, Peregrine, M. (2023). Davos obsession with 'polycrisis' may seem remote, but corporate boards should take notice. *Forbes*, 20 January. Miliband, D. (2023). Our age of impunity. *New York Times*, 17 February. Drezner, D. (2023). Are we headed toward a 'polycrisis'? The buzzword of the moment, explained. *Vox*, 28 January. Kluth, A. (2023). So we're in a polycrisis. Is that even a thing? *Washington Post*, 21 January. UNDP (2022). Polycrisis and long-term thinking. Report, 31 August (https://www.undp.org/asia-pacific/publications/polycrisis-and-long-term-thinking-reimagining-development-asia-and-pacific-foresight-brief).

5 See, for example, Chapagain, J. (2022). Hope in the midst of hopelessness. Report, 10 July, IFRC (https://www.ifrc.org/article/ifrc-secretary-general-year-ahead-hope-midst-hopelessness). See also Lawrence, M., *et al.* (2022). What is a global polycrisis? Report, 16 September, Cascade Institute (https://cascadeinstitute.org/wp-content/uploads/2022/04/What-is-a-global-polycrisis-v2.pdf).

6 Serhan, Y. (2023). Why 'polycrisis' was the buzzword of day 1 in Davos. *Time*, 17 January. Torkington, S. (2023). We're on the brink of a 'polycrisis' – how worried should we be? World Economic Forum, 13 January.

7 See centre-right think thank Bright Blue's advocacy of carbon taxes: Buckland, J. (2021). Green money: a plan to reform UK carbon pricing. Report, Bright Blue (www.brightblue.org.uk/portfolio/green-money-a-plan-to-reform-uk-carbon-pricing/). See also Lord Deben (John Gummer) in the *New Statesman*: Gummer, J. (2022). On the climate crisis, to delay is to deny. *New Statesman*, 31 October (www.newstatesman.com/spotlight/sustainability/energy/2022/10/cop27-climate-crisis-delay-deny-john-gummer).

8   See Anderson, K. (2016). The trouble with negative emissions. *Science* 354:182–183   (www.science.org/doi/10.1126/science.aah4567).   See also Anderson, K., *et al.* (2020). A factor of two: how the mitigation plans of 'climate progressive' nations fall far short of Paris-compliant pathways. *Climate Policy* 20(10):1,290–1,304 (DOI: 10.1080/146930 62.2020.1728209). Or a more recent interview at www.kontext-tv.de/en/Kevin_Anderson_Climate_Targets.

9   See https://signon.scientistrebellion.com/.

10   See, for example, Hassol, S., and Mann, M. (2022). Now is not the time to give in to climate fatalism. *Time*, 12 April (https://time.com/6166123/climate-change-fatalism/). Tigue, K. (2022). 'Doomism' or reality? Divided over its message, the climate movement seeks balance. *Inside Climate News*, 17 June (https://insideclimatenews.org/news/17062022/doomism-or-reality-divided-over-its-message-the-climate-movement-seeks-balance/). Richardson, J. A. (2015). When the end of human civilization is your day job. *Esquire Magazine* (www.esquire.com/news-politics/a36228/ballad-of-the-sad-climatologists-0815/).

11   Whitmarsh, L., *et al.* (2022). Climate anxiety: what predicts it and how is it related to climate action? *Journal of Environmental Psychology* 83:101866.

12   See, for example, Marks, E., *et al.* (2021). Young people's voices on climate anxiety, government betrayal and moral injury: a global phenomenon. Preprint, SSRN, 7 September.

13   We note that Unger does not see climate breakdown as a serious threat, but this does not undermine his relevance here.

14   McCormick, E. (2022). Patagonia's billionaire owner gives away company to fight climate crisis. *The Guardian*, 14 September (www.theguardian.com/us-news/2022/sep/14/patagonias-billionaire-owner-gives-away-company-to-fight-climate-crisis-yvon-chouinard).

15   Wang, S., Corner, A., and Nicholls, J. (2020). Britain Talks Climate: a toolkit for engaging the British public on climate change. Report, 18 November (https://climateoutreach.org/reports/britain-talks-climate/).

16   Ibid.

17   See, for example, Food and Agriculture Organization of the United Nations (2019). The biodiversity that is crucial for our food and agriculture is disappearing by the day. Article, 22 February (www.fao.

org/news/story/en/item/1180463/icode/). Mace, G. M., Barrett, M., Burgess, N. D., *et al.* (2018). Aiming higher to bend the curve of biodiversity loss. *Nature Sustainability* 1:448–451 (https://doi.org/10.1038/s41893-018-0130-0).

18 Read, R. (2017). Thrutopia. *Huffington Post*, 6 November (www.huffingtonpost.co.uk/rupert-read/thrutopia-why-neither-dys_b_18372090.html).

19 Bielskyte, M. (2023). Forget utopia. Ignore dystopia. Embrace protopia! *New York Times*, 14 March (www.nytimes.com/2023/03/14/special-series/protopia-movement.html).

PART III

ACTIVATION

making them happen

CHAPTER 4

'What can I do?' Two pillars of citizen action

Rupert Read and Rosie Bell

The climate movement the world needs will eventually be as big as any war effort. It will be created by millions of people, from many backgrounds, with unique needs and talents. As we have discussed, such an emergent movement is unpredictable and unplannable. However, it is still necessary and possible to offer meaningful support to the citizen who duly shows up asking: 'What can I do?'

While we cannot prescribe people's actions, we *can* point to certain domains of human life in which people are already organizing serious, inspiring climate action of the kind that we believe can ultimately constitute a powerful mass movement. These tend to be the areas where people already exercise a good deal of their everyday power together, to whatever end. While they in no way represent the limits of possibility for citizen action, we explore here two very important arenas of collective agency in which people are most likely find their own place in the climate movement: the world of work and the geographic community. Building on the brief introduction in chapter 3, this chapter offers an overview of how citizen action in these areas can underpin institutional transformation. The guest chapters that follow introduce just a handful of the many initiatives that are already leading the way – in the words of the people that are making them happen.

Work and climate

Wherever people spend their collective energy performing critical functions of institutions and systems often lies their greatest potential to effect system *change*. The world of work therefore represents a crucial pillar of the mass-climate-movement-in-waiting. For better or worse, work is where many of us spend most of our active lives. The greatest proportion of our collective endeavour is invested here, channelled into societal and ecological impact of one kind or another – deliberately or otherwise. From the corridors of global power and the executive boardroom to the school canteen and the factory floor, work is the most active means of our participation in a (fracturing) socioeconomic system. For many of us, the implicit power that this represents is considerably greater than that afforded by a vote in a first-past-the-post electoral system. The climate movement must now find ways to harness the formidable resource that is working life, in the service of positive change.

It is not only our power that is embedded in the world of work. Entangled in the organizations that keep the growth economy spinning are the processes and dependencies responsible for extractive and exploitative practices, and for most man-made carbon emissions. Transformation within and around organizations, considered at scale and activated with determination, can have a vast impact on environmental factors. At an employee level, despite shifts away from workers' rights and unionized protections towards a precarious gig economy, the fact remains that everything accomplished by organizations (and the societal structures they maintain) depends on people at work. Many people are still well positioned to bring change 'entrepreneurially', pressing for concessions from decision makers with the implicit leverage of withdrawing labour where protections do exist. As the UN Environment Programme points out, trade unions are in a unique position to highlight the relationship between the climate crisis and employment, to advocate for mitigation and adaptation initiatives in both the public and private sectors, and to mobilize and support employees to participate.[1] Scope exists for far more unions to become serious about a just transition from an extractive to a regenerative economy.

The varieties of possible action are endless: from localized, shallow leverage points, to more deeply transformational, sector-wide initiatives and efforts to transform the legislative context in which business operates. For example, employees may influence the ecological footprint of their physical workplace, from insulating premises and switching energy suppliers to challenging aspects of procurement and supply chains. They might question how employers discourage or encourage climate action from employees or from other companies. They could shine a light on how profits are invested – ethically or otherwise – or take an interest in how companies affect the world through their advertising practices, brand identity and lobbying activities.

Every organization and sector has a unique relationship with the crisis, representing a unique and important channel of impact. For example, what if a company such as Amazon chose to take a stand against climate-denialist content? Could more human resources bodies seek out climate-positive pension plans? Could healthcare professionals – understanding the links between access to green space and physical and mental health – persuade the NHS to prioritize rewilding and 'green gyms' on the cumulatively vast green spaces around hospitals, as part of a holistic approach to health and ecology? What if bodies of professionals – lawyers, accountants, insurers, marketeers – stood together to influence their corporate employers and clients against greenwashing and insisted on real responsibility? What if they withheld their services from clients that failed to demonstrate transformative action, or from those that oppose serious government action on climate and nature. What would happen if they lent their professional weight and financial support to effective climate initiatives?

More often than we might think, taking workplace climate action does not ask us to blow against the wind but rather to lean into change as current crises continue to destabilize business as usual. For example, as the post-Covid world continues to consider its working future, there is important scope for employee-led transformation where old structures and inertias have been uprooted.

Perhaps the most obvious area to address is our approach to location and transport. The upheaval of the pandemic revealed untold potential for shifting working locations. Lockdowns and restrictions enforced a massive reduction in commuting and in overseas business travel, accelerating a wholesale upgrade of the digital infrastructure that facilitates home working on a global scale. While home working brings challenges as well as freedoms, precedent now exists for a transformed working life wherein precious travel hours are restored to workers, transport emissions are reduced, and the case for maintaining unsustainable business premises is called into question. What is more, the vulnerabilities of our current transport system have been laid bare by recent disruption in global energy markets. In combination, these factors contribute to a strong business case for a shift not only towards electrified transport, but also towards *less* travel and thus reduced energy demand.

All such impacts are merely dress rehearsals for the climate-driven disruption and supply shocks that are to come. Business owners may expect that ongoing instability and rising prices will impact their operations at different points in supply and production for the rest of their working lives. In the interest of future-proofing, therefore, they may feel the wisdom of greater localization, which would entail both less commuting and also shorter and less resource-intensive supply lines. Indeed, the only prediction that businesses can make with any certainty is that of *un*certainty, and this is true in areas beyond transport too. The companies that survive will be those that learn to let go of outdated practices in an increasingly unpredictable world.

Creating a sustainable playing field

Climate-positive initiatives within organizations contribute directly to sustainability goals, and they can also signal to policymakers that appetite for change exists at an institutional level. But in terms of scale, the most powerful lever that employees can use is their ability to make the climate matter to corporations, and matter enough for them to support decarbonization measures at the level of lobbying and public policy.

Bill Weihl, founder of the US-based organization ClimateVoice, urges workers to learn from the grassroots mainstreaming of LGBT rights in the US from within corporations, who went from being bystanders to 'upstanders' in this political space thanks to organized pressure from their employees.[2] Political inaction on climate is currently maintained in part by grossly disproportionate fossil fuel lobbying, powerful enough to fatally dampen large-scale climate action and investment from policymakers. But Weihl perceives a latent antidote in the muscle of other corporates who remain silent on climate because a stance of 'neutrality' suits their bottom line. It is within the power of employees to renegotiate this relationship between company and climate, organizing internally and coordinating with external groups to pressure leaders to make it their business. If corporations are thus persuaded to shoulder responsibility and use their influence in the policy space, their active intervention could help balance out the most stubborn barriers to rapid, effective decarbonization policies at the highest political level.

Lobbying should place significant focus on changes to business law itself, with the goal being a switch among responsible corporates from advocating regulatory exemptions and lower taxes to seeking better and more stringent sustainability regulation that can hold all businesses to account, driving out climate bad actors. Business (including finance) has immense power to lead such changes. As our theory of change reports, conversations with a wide range of businesspeople reveal a surprising level of openness to these ideas. Making the journey from openness to action will require pressure from clients, employees and customers alike.

ACTION ACCORDING TO CAPACITY

The suggestion that aspects of employment be used as leverage in collective bargaining carries an obvious political charge, and it could invite criticism from those eager to cast the climate movement as somehow an 'elitist' project. For some, the idea of creating disruption at work triggers similar alarm bells to that of risking arrest – these interventions, designed with people who are relatively secure and comfortable in mind, can expose those in a position of oppression to greater risk. It is important, then, to emphasize both the spectrum of possibility within workplace action and the onus on individuals to do what is within their power to do, alongside others. Above we imagined just a handful of the activities that, with commitment and at scale, could help transform the political economy from within the space of our employment. They are diverse in their access points, impact and reach, and so are the workers who can initiate and implement them. Among their number are qualified, affluent, unionized professionals on one side, a squeezed and vulnerable precariat on the other, and everybody in between. In some workplaces, therefore, action will be led by unions; in others, by professional associations, by small groups of concerned workers, or by managers or owners; and in many, hopefully, by all of these stakeholders collaboratively.

In such a distributed, context-specific mobilization, citizens may reach for whichever facet of action makes most sense in their own circumstances and within the bounds of their own empowerment, without any obligation to compromise their survival needs. An inclusive climate movement demands this: people need inspiration to step forward without being pushed beyond what is materially possible or safe. Importantly, however, where protections do exist, workers have the power to withdraw their labour – symbolically or otherwise – if their reasonable demands are resisted. This is the approach pioneered by the grassroots movement Earth Strike,[3] and encouragingly it is starting to attract interest from some trade unions. Workers who benefit from protections are also in a position to normalize climate strike measures, potentially widening the space of possibility for less empowered employees to participate in future action.

Across the mainstream political spectrum it is still all-too-common to cast corporate-focused climate action as a threat to job security. Commitments to emissions reduction are still met with firm resistance from certain trade unions, and, at the time of writing, the Labour Party's plans for ambitious investment in green industry and, in particular, for a moratorium on new North Sea oil licences have been scaled back in response to pressure from major unions.[4] To counter this kind of catastrophic short-term thinking from within the field of employment protection, we must combine emphasis on the good economic sense of climate mitigation and adaptation with the truth that we cannot go on playing today's jobs off against tomorrow's liveable world. Attempts to protect jobs by preserving the status quo fail on their own terms if business-as-usual destabilizes the planet in the near-to-medium term.

Furthermore, jobs in areas of high carbon emissions are those most likely to be lost if workers do not themselves participate in leading the coming transition towards just outcomes.[5] Society has long associated work with the concept of building a future, and that future must now once again be given priority. For many of us, our labour remains the best source of our power to protect that future.

EMERGING EXAMPLES

A number of US-based organizations offer valuable templates for workplace organizing. Among them is the already-mentioned ClimateVoice, which is focused specifically on 'the hidden power of companies to change the game on climate'.[6] Its broad-based approach includes both direct campaigns aimed at corporates and empowerment of employees to catalyse advocacy from their employers, helping drive policy change.

Here in the UK, the promising initiative Honest Work seeks to help workers change their companies across the English-speaking world.[7] Already in the Climate Majority Project incubator, Lawyers for Net Zero offers an impressive example of sector-wide organizing. This growing network of law professionals focuses on the potential for in-house senior counsel to help corporations avoid greenwashing and achieve legitimate net zero. Adam Woodhall, the organization's founder, won Nexis 'Legal Personality of the Year' in 2023: a strong indicator of the wide appeal and backing that profession-based networks can generate, far beyond the climate bubble. Other groups are emerging in key domains such as insurance, health and more.

In these areas and countless others, workplace climate action now requires the energy and attention of millions of climate-concerned people. For some, this will be as simple as joining an existing group. Others will find they need to self-organize, following either emerging examples or the growing body of work that provides would-be-actors with the tools they need to have an impact. Among the most impressive resources available in this space is Paul Hawken's Project Drawdown, which offers, among other things, a by-sector framework of learning resources and practical interventions for rapid, safe and equitable emissions drawdown for cities, classrooms and policymakers.[8] Drawdown Labs spearheads efforts to scale these solutions in the private sector, and it has recently published a how-to guide for employees pushing for sweeping climate action from their employers.[9] Hawken is likewise responsible for Project Regeneration, whose Regeneration Nexus provides accessible, practical, regenerative climate solutions and access points for everyone from the classroom to the boardroom, at individual, group and company levels.[10]

Leaning on an open door?

Companies know that action is coming. A recent survey of 375 global executives found that four in five foresee an 'unprecedented rise in workplace activism' in the coming years, with sustainability and climate an increasing focus of concern.[11] Employers are beginning to understand that the demands of purpose-driven millennial and Generation Z employee bases will reshape workplaces and society.[12] While some organizations would prefer internal activism to go away and are punitive in their approaches,[13] others are prepared to respond in the interest of their own resilience – that is, to head off the growing trend of 'conscious quitting'. In the UK, recent studies have revealed that 83% of workers believe their workplaces are not doing enough to address the climate challenge, and employees are beginning to vote with their feet, choosing – where possible – to lend their power to companies with stronger environmental policies.[14] Students at top UK universities recently announced a 'career boycott' of major insurers, pledging not to work for certain firms if they continued to support controversial fossil fuel projects.[15]

Accordingly, employee demands have been identified as a major driver of Fortune 500 decarbonization commitments.[16] In response to these patterns, frameworks for sustainable system change are evolving within and around organizations. Innovators are responding with toolkits and roadmaps for companies to embrace meaningful sustainability changes across their activities.[17] We may take heart from such initiatives while understanding that the required shift has only just begun. In a short space of time we must step fully into the space that is being opened, escalating demand and ensuring that these trickles of encouragement become a landslide.

Importantly, as multiple crises impact organizations and the contexts in which they operate, workplace activation need not necessarily be a source of conflict and antagonism, or even a matter of force. As leaders negotiate the challenges of our complex and volatile world, many climate-positive changes make good business sense. While for certain organizations it would be naive to imply that transformation towards sustainability is even possible within recognizable business models, many others are already aware that capacity for change is the only route to survival amid current crises. Business as usual makes less and less sense in this rapidly shifting landscape, and organizational change is itself a burgeoning industry. What is more, in many cases the *type* of change advocated by experts tends towards better understanding of the systemic relationships in which organizations are embedded. Whereas many of the world's intersecting crises originate in disregard of complexity on the part of companies, industries and governments,[18] these same crises – and Covid-19 in particular – have catalysed a shift in this view. Many leaders now demonstrate willingness to look beyond their own isolated priorities and understand their operations within interconnected systems. This parallel appetite for change, for resilience and for systems thinking creates a fertile context for internal actors to demonstrate alignment between the long-term needs of an industry or sector and strong, pragmatic action on climate.

ACTION IN LOCAL COMMUNITIES

'The world is on everyone's doorstep and has to be reckoned with.' — Indra Adnan, *The Politics of Waking Up*

At the same time as climate-concerned citizens are beginning to realize their power in the workplace, a second pillar of climate action is coalescing around a different but perhaps equally potent locus of citizen agency: the geographic community.

In a social world that is increasingly mediated by digital interaction and further fragmented by the effects of the pandemic, many of us are sorely disconnected from even our closest local areas. Our insulation from each other both contributes to the alienation and poor mental health that drive mass unsustainable consumption and cuts us off from our extraordinary collective power to create the world we wish to see. But where we are physically together, we can *act* together to change ways of life at all sorts of scales. In real-life communities, we are empowered not only to demand change, outsourcing responsibility to slow-moving, ambivalent centralized government, but also to participate in and co-create actual climate responses ourselves. We can enact sustainable behaviour changes locally, embedding regenerative practices and collaborating towards building more resilient and appropriate systems. Localized solutions challenge the dangerous, false belief that we have to wait for our leaders to agree what to do about climate decline and nature decline. They grow from the understanding that many of the necessary tools are already here, and we are free to pick them up and use them.

Scale and complexity can make the concept of 'the climate crisis' hard to grasp and engage with. By contrast, locally embedded initiatives can bring enfranchisement in the climate movement by allowing people to link environmental issues with the real needs and challenges of daily life. From building- and land-use change to local food production and transport initiatives, the retrofitting of homes, mutual aid, energy generation, waste reduction, urban green space and rewilding, technology sharing and circular economies, climate action in communities brings a planetary cause home to where we are. In doing so, as we will discuss, it also allows us to overcome the feelings of hopelessness and polarization that hamper meaningful action on climate, and to address directly the crises of meaning and relationship that drive environmental destruction.

'You never change things by fighting the existing reality. To change something, build a new model that makes the existing model obsolete.' — Buckminster Fuller, systems theorist

Healthy and robust climate action in local communities does not necessarily focus on 'climate' as the only or ultimate value of concern.[19] The most effective local solutions are often embedded in other material needs and pragmatic concerns. These include the new forms of localized self-organization arising amid the slow-motion breakdown of our current systems. From jobs to housing and food, where exploitative, extractive, short-sighted central government has left local communities deprived and disempowered across multiple dimensions of civic life, fertile ground exists for grassroots organizing driven by the unique concerns and energies of people on the ground. Such initiatives are diverse, place specific and already happening. Chapters 5 and 7 explore some flourishing examples: namely the Community Climate Action Project and local climate hubs.[20]

Many local initiatives fulfil the definition of 'commoning': the organization of shared 'resources' – such as land, water and food systems or infrastructure and technology – by and for a coherent group; and the protocols and values devised by the community to manage and protect the commons for collective benefit.[21] It would be a grave mistake to dismiss such local initiatives as being too small to make a difference. Conversely, to leap to the question of how such activity might be 'scaled' is to risk cutting off the source of its power: grassroots, localized agency. Advocates of commoning approach the relationship between small localized initiatives and system change at scale via a fractal model, wherein commoners emulate each other's practices and form larger networks and collaborative systems. The commoning model therefore presents a blueprint and a natural ally for a localized, distributed climate movement with a joined-up impact.

In a similar way, the founders of the political platform The Alternative UK offer a 'cosmo-local' vision (and framework) for realizing the power of emergent local organizing through fractal replication. Indra Adnan's advocacy of CANs (which can stand for Citizen Action Networks, Community Agency Networks or Climate Action Networks) highlights the potential for planetary impact through networks of decentralized, local, action-based solutions to multiple interlocking crises.[22] Operating at the personal, societal and planetary levels, CANs are simultaneously places where citizens can participate in solutions as communities; civil society entities with political agency among other local, national and global organizations; and direct routes to decarbonization that bypass the procrastination of central government. Among Adnan's most important insights from the process of designing and prototyping CANs has been her encouraging discovery that they already exist. In communities across the world, particularly in the wake of Covid-19, self-organizing groups of local people are connecting with each other, linking local needs with collective wisdom, and working to envision new systems.[23]

Organizations such as The Alternative UK and the Commons Strategies Group offer rigorous frameworks for understanding how action-based solutions in local communities can be a source of emergent solutions at the societal and planetary levels. But unlike top-down, technocratic policies that lack popular appeal and leave ordinary people outside the equation, these practices are real, familiar and accessible. The community work we want to support belongs within and beside these existing and emerging models for civic agency. It is rooted in the needs and opportunities experienced by real communities, and it innovates, imitates and multiplies remedies that are appropriate to people and place.

This fundamentally accessible strand of citizen climate action aligns with 'radical' goals without needing to impose radical ideology. It challenges existing social structures at a deep level without requiring participants to sign up to an explicit doctrine of tearing down the system. From a place of creativity and regeneration rather than antagonism or destruction, it purposefully builds what is needed, where it is needed. At the same time as increasing local autonomy, it reduces reliance on central institutions, syphoning power away from a disintegrating system. The Alternative UK therefore builds on the work of Václav Benda and others in imagining a 'Parallel Polis', wherein citizens cocreate supplementary socioeconomic–political architecture, changing the shape of the state and its power from outside.[24]

Climate action in local communities can propagate not only through new networks but also through existing groups whose values incline towards protection of humanity and the more-than-human. Important among these are faith groups, ever more of whom recognize their leadership role in stewarding the living world, and underlining its relationship with the sacred. In the UK, for example, the Islamic Foundation for Ecology and Environmental Sciences works 'to develop ecological knowledge and promote conservation and sustainable development based on environmental ethics contained in

Islamic teachings'. Faith for the Climate Network brings together religious leaders of many faiths in thought leadership to support communities' climate response. Beyond traditional faith groups, our environmental crisis is increasingly perceived as rooted in the inner world (see chapter 13), and as the climate movement continues to grow, it is likely (and desirable) that 'eco-spiritual' understanding will become an ever more widespread motivator of action.

Reconnecting inside and out

Our need for regeneration in geographic communities goes beyond the ecological and even the political. The Covid-19 lockdowns worsened an already-serious trend towards physical isolation and the fragmentation of communities. In our powerfully absorbing digital spaces we have learned to replace quality of connection with quantity of connection, our increasing anxiety reflecting the time and social energies that are consumed by many shallow interactions at the expense of deeper relationships. We devote ever more of our time and attention to virtual communities that do not serve our physical and societal needs. At the same time, unaccustomed to perceiving our part in a far larger whole, many of us are unable to see how we might have a role to play in bringing change. Tangible, local, collaborative action is the essence of what we have lost in recent decades, and working together towards common goals of resilience, preparedness and sustainability is not only a survival necessity but a route back towards the deeper sense of interdependency we so badly need.

Similarly, the polarization that tears society apart and that can bracket climate action as a matter of 'green ideology' is, in many ways, a function of lives lived online. Hardened against each other's (perceived) views by digital manipulation, we are divorced from our embodied sense of 'other' people as three dimensional, human and relatable. We may theorize about polarization and warn against it all we like, but its best antidote is the medicine of other people, and the shared work that allows us to enact connection, and thus come to understand that there is more that unites us than divides us. Chapters 5 and 7 outline heartening ways in which initiatives for climate action can help to strengthen community.

Finally, it is important – as always – to note that all practical climate action begins in conversation, and therefore in community, near and far. While we may feel an urgency to move beyond words to deeds, the most effective first step any of us can take is to connect with the others who share our concerns and start a conversation. Many potentially influential groups lack a sense of connectedness in the face of the climate threat, and as such they are unaware of their collective power. As our guest authors colourfully demonstrate, empowering individuals through inclusion in wider conversations can unlock their agency. Such a conversation requires bonds of community to be repaired and nurtured – and its cultivation strengthens those bonds in turn.

TRANSFORMATIVE ADAPTATION

The concept of transformative adaptation provides another valuable perspective on local climate action. Originating in academia and the United Nations, it refers to adaptation efforts that seek significant local transformation to address root causes of vulnerability.[25] This approach goes beyond incremental and defensive approaches (shallow adaptation) while stopping short of complete collapse readiness (deep adaptation).

Transformative Adaptation (TrAd) is also the name of a British community of mainly former XR activists.[26] TrAd functions as a 'moderate flank' to both XR and the Deep Adaptation Forum, building on the widespread increase in climate consciousness and a desire to act, while accepting that it is now too late to merely 'mitigate' our way out of climate breakdown and that some harms are now inevitable. Its activities comprise thought leadership and small-scale experiments on the ground, both temporary (e.g. the 'TrAd village' onsite at the annual Green Gathering Festival) and ongoing at dwellings and eco-villages around the country.[27] TrAd operates on the understanding that there will be no 'new normal', but rather a constant reactive and proactive pattern of change. Far from advocating doomism, however, TrAd is a framework for embracing and making the best of that process, rather than fighting the inevitable.

Climate action in communities that embodies transformative adaptation, e.g. water storage and local food resiliency initiatives, is critical in raising climate consciousness more generally. When we are exposed to practical initiatives in our own communities that respond to transformed circumstances, and that are prepared to cope with further waves of climate damage, the reality of our shared situation is brought home. The benefits of community action on climate go beyond the immediate and practical, becoming a permanent wake-up call.

*

This chapter has introduced two important channels of citizen energy that can be activated for climate. But workplaces and geographic communities are far from the only routes to citizen action. The chapters that follow feature voices from emerging initiatives across a number of impact areas, some of whom are also part of the Climate Majority Project incubator. While this small selection captures imperfectly the breadth of citizen work emerging across the country, we are grateful to the innovators who took the time to share their journeys to climate action and to discuss the strategies behind their compelling initiatives. Theirs are the kinds of idea that, with sufficient support to build scale, have the potential to change the trajectory of the climate story, supplying citizens with meaningful ways to use their collective power. By amplifying their stories we hope to provide inspiration for many more such projects to emerge and flourish.

NOTES

1   See UN Environment Programme (2008). Climate change, its consequences on employment and trade union action: a training manual for workers and trade unions. Report (https://wedocs.unep.org/bitstream/handle/20.500.11822/8570/TOT_ClimateChangeManual_eng.pdf?sequence=3&amp%3BisAllowed=).
2   Weill, B. (2021). The hidden power of companies to change the game on climate. YouTube (https://www.youtube.com/watch?v=BtdCuRjr0B4).
3   See https://earth-strike.co.uk/.

4   See, for example, Quinn, B. (2023). Labour plans to ban North Sea oil production naive, says union leader. *The Guardian*, 4 June (www. theguardian.com/politics/2023/jun/04/labour-plans-to-ban-north-sea-oil-production-naive-says-union-leader).

5   Thus the Biden administration's huge investment in green jobs, in its ambitious 'Inflation Reduction Act' commitments to a kind of Green New Deal. Britain risks falling far behind in its out-of-date (lack of) industrial policy.

6   See https://honestwork.org/about/about-honest-work/.

7   See https://honestwork.org/what-to-change/overview/.

8   See https://drawdown.org/drawdown-framework.

9   See https://drawdown.org/publications/climate-solutions-at-work.

10 See https://regeneration.org/nexus.

11 Sax, S. (2020). Employees are fighting for a new cause at work: the climate. *HuffPost*, 27 April (www.ecowatch.com/employee-climate-activism-2645855023.html).

12 Robison, J. (2019). Millennials worry about the environment – should your company? *Gallup* (www.gallup.com/workplace/257786/millenni als-worry-environment-company.aspx).

13 Hillsdon, M. (2022). Society watch: the rise of employee climate activism. *Reuters* (www.reutersevents.com/sustainability/society-watch-rise -employee-climate-activism).

14 Acaroglu, L. (2020). Employees want climate-positive action from companies. Here's how they can deliver. *Reuters* (www.reutersevents. com/sustainability/employees-want-climate-positive-action-compani es-heres-how-they-can-deliver).

15 Makortoff, K. (2023). UK students pledge 'career boycott' of insurers over fossil fuels. *The Guardian*, 24 May (www.theguardian.com/busi ness/2023/may/24/uk-students-pledge-career-boycott-of-insurers-over -fossil-fuels).

16 Climate Impact Partners (2022). Fortune Global 500 climate commitments. Report (www.naturalcapitalpartners.com/news/article/dee ds-not-words-new-research-reveals-the-climate-action-of-fortune-500 -glob).

17 Acaroglu, L. (2020). Employees want climate-positive action from companies. Here's how they can deliver. *Reuters* (www.reutersevents. com/sustainability/employees-want-climate-positive-action-compa-nies-heres-how-they-can-deliver).

18 See, for example, Bjorkman, T. (2018). How to use personal, inner development to build strong democracies. TEDxBerlin (www.youtube.com/watch?time_ continue=92&v=b4dFsHgd1rQ&feature=emb_logo).

19 Although as the weather starts to brings the realities of the crisis home, local impacts become a driving force even in the (so far) temperate UK.

20 The Climate Majority Project is working to convene highly effective initiatives in this space to share best practice, and to expand awareness that inclusive mobilization is underway in local communities (see chapter 3).

21 Adapted with thanks from Bollier, D. (2022). Commoning and changemaking. Essay, Schumacher Center for a New Economics (https://centerforneweconomics.org/publications/commoning-and-changemaking).

22 See The Alternative's website at www.thealternative.org.uk/citizens-action-network. See also www.greens-can.Earth.

23 Cape Town Community Action Networks present a particularly striking parallel. See, for example, Writers' Community Action Network (2020). Cape Town Together: organizing in a city of islands. *Roar Magazine*, 5 June (https://roarmag.org/essays/cape-town-together-organizing-in-a-city-of-islands/).

24 Adnan, I. (2021). *The Politics of Waking Up*. Perspectiva.

25 See, for example, Fedele, G., Donatti, C. I., Harvey, C. A., Hannah, L., Hole, D. G. (2019). Transformative adaptation to climate change for sustainable social-ecological systems. *Environmental Science & Policy* 101:116–125.

26 See www.transformative-adaptation.com.

27 A book about TrAd edited by Morgan Phillips and Rupert Read is forthcoming from Permanent Press in 2024. *Facing Up to Climate Reality: Honesty, Disaster and Hope* (2019, ed. J. Foster, Green House Publishing/London Publishing Partnership) offers in-depth treatment of transformative adaptation, urging a responsive and adaptive stance towards a future characterized by continuous and significant change owing to destabilized systems.

CHAPTER 5

Community Climate Action: what you do right now matters

Joolz Thompson

Half a century of inaction on the climate and ecological emergency means our communities must now take sustainability measures into their own hands. Leaders must act, of course, and there is 'only so much' communities can do, but 'change is rarely a gift from above':[1] we urgently need to come together and build resilience in the face of an uncertain future. Community Climate Action provides the skills, software, knowledge and consultancy needed to enable neighbourhoods to write and enact a local Climate Action Plan – by the people, for the people. Its methodologies are scalable, popular and coming soon to a parish near you.

I was three years old when ozone depletion was hypothesized, and twelve when it became scientific consensus. That year, twenty nations signed the Vienna Convention for the Protection of the Ozone Layer.[2] Two years later, signatories of the Montreal Protocol began phasing out production and use of substances causing ozone depletion.[3] I may not live to see the ozone layer fully healed, but by the age of fourteen I had witnessed widespread public concern and scientific consensus leading to swift international action to keep people and the planet safe.

You might therefore excuse me if I thought governments around the world would act with the same immediacy to the threat of climate change!

This crisis has been a constant throughout my life. Before I was born, the 1965 President's Science Advisory Committee Report on Atmospheric Carbon Dioxide called the greenhouse effect a matter of 'real concern'.[4] When I was two, the term 'global warming' was first used in the title of a scientific paper. I was fifteen when the IPCC was founded and sixteen when Margaret Thatcher spoke to the UN about atmospheric CO_2, calling for a global treaty. At nineteen I witnessed the Rio Earth Summit.[5] At twenty-four (when my daughter was two), the Kyoto Protocol was agreed.[6] I was thirty-three when *The Stern Review* found that curbing climate change would cost around 1% of global gross domestic product (GDP), while failing to do so would cost around 20%.[7] Threaten the economy, and there's bound to be action, right? When the Paris Agreement[8] – a legally binding international treaty, with 194 parties – was signed, I was forty-two and my daughter was twenty. This problem is definitely going to be fixed. Right?

Meanwhile, as we know, dangerous emissions and global temperatures have increased steadily. We are expected to pass warming of 1.5°C in the next decade; some predict that will happen as early as 2024.[9] Our parliament, local authorities and cities have declared an emergency, but despite devastating climate impacts, the onset of resource wars and economic warfare around fossil fuels – not to mention the risk that irreversible tipping points may soon be reached – the UK government fails to act appropriately. It pledges to fight climate change in one breath while greenlighting new coal mines and fossil fuel licences in another. I am now forty-nine. My daughter is twenty-seven. I know now that I will never see an end to this. The world will not be healed or know safety again. This is not going to be another ozone layer: our governments are not coming to save us this time.

As a citizen, it is easy to be stunned into inaction. The magnitude of this wicked problem is hard to comprehend. When you do grasp our reality, it is easy to understand why some might choose civil disobedience. It is a logical response to demand that governments take action: I did. I have petitioned, written letters, protested, voted and marched. Much has been achieved through direct action, and climate movements and protests are growing. They have influenced public opinion – but not enough. Not in time. So what can we do?

It starts with bringing climate stories *home.*

Community Climate Action: how communities can change the world

The past seven years were the hottest on record in the green-and-pleasant UK.[10] Summer 2022 saw extreme heat and drought. At the time of writing, as El Niño kicks in, summer 2023 is seeing even more records break. Ahead of us are water shortages, crop failures, a decline in biodiversity and rising pollution.[11] We will see more chemicals and sewage in our rivers and streams, the fundamental eradication of soil fertility,[12] and 'day zero' in UK cities, where demand for water outstrips supply. Rising food and energy prices will be accompanied by more extremes of heat and cold; more drought, fires and flooding.

As Carl Sagan said: 'Anything else you're interested in isn't going to happen if you can't breathe the air and drink the water. Don't sit this one out. Do something.'

I always thought he was right – somebody *should* do something. The moment I realized that actually I am that somebody, I shifted my energy from complaint (protest and civil disobedience) to action. If the government is not coming to save us, then we will take the care of people and the planet into our own hands to adapt to our new reality – in our communities, with the people nearest to us.

The solutions are available, we just need collective action to implement them together

It is our civic duty to grow community resilience in the face of crises, by way of mutual aid, and this is a concept we are all on board with since the Covid-19 pandemic. And yes, let's 'Insulate Britain', but we shouldn't stop at insulating or retrofitting our houses. Let's have renewable community energy, greater biodiversity, resilient food systems and clean water, and let's establish the institutions, expertise, funding and finance to deliver them, locally. By the people, for the people: community owned and democratically controlled.

Community Climate Action formed as an organization around our experiments with these ideas in my own Suffolk community. Local and government climate action plans vary in quality, but most are inadequate, and I wanted to empower people to come together locally and figure it out themselves. Self-determination is vital: don't wait; don't ask permission to prepare your own community for the climate consequences that are coming. Start talking to each other about what you can do.

Our own conversation started around a campfire. A group of friends – festival crew, skilled in building transient environments, unsustainably. We asked each other: how can we use our productive activity to impact environments permanently ... and sustainably?

We set out not with a comprehensive plan but with a series of actions. We bought ten acres of land for market gardening and took on the local pub as a climate hub; we wanted it to become an example retrofit and the cornerstone of a smart energy microgrid. (It now also functions as an all-important gathering place for the community to communicate about what is at stake.) We launched community composting and waste programmes, we began testing rainwater capture and reed bed filtration systems for waste and toxic run-off water, and we started planting trees to mitigate flooding. We met to discuss 'degrowth': what might that mean for our community? How do we consume less and share more?

As the director of a community benefit society, I began attending parish council meetings and learned a lot about how power is wielded locally – particularly the power of these councils to influence how public money is spent via the district and county councillors in attendance. Parish councils are powerful. And most parishes have an emergency plan: what to do if there is some kind of disaster. We need to update those emergency plans in line with the climate and ecological emergency. We have climate emergency declarations at the district and county levels, but their targets become more unrealistic with each passing month and county councils are unable to make laws. Also, they have no money. The impetus for change has to come from below – councils will not be able to get any of this done if local communities are not on board. So an idea was born. Why not write a community climate action plan, in support of our district and county targets?

We put the proposition in front of our parish council, and the motion was passed as part of a lottery bid under the title 'Together for Our Planet'. Local interest snowballed, and we have since become a 'green cluster' of six parish councils, with two more on the way. We have also been joined by other local food producers, community groups, conservation groups and, most importantly, our local Farm Cluster (as featured in the BBC's *Save Our Wild Isles*). We set out from the beginning to empower people to create their *own* plans through a sequence of participatory workshops – deliberative democracy in action. Writing a plan gives people ownership and a sense of pride in place – civic duty, even. (I had to bite my tongue firmly to avoid influencing the conversation.) Setting aside political differences we came up with a set of goals based on values that we all had: kindness and sharing; availability of clean air and water; access to good housing. In the process of coming up with these values it was continually clear that there is more to unite than to divide us.

Reviewers of the lottery bid said it was one of the best they had ever received, because it was *replicable* and *scalable* and *left a legacy*. This scalability is everything when you are looking at creating real impact from below. We are currently in conversation with the Society for Local Council Clerks – representing 5,000 councils – about widening the programme. Soon, thousands of communities just like ours should be able to use our methodology to write their own locally appropriate plans for climate action.

Rebuilding the commons – and attracting the funds

Many local climate solutions bring benefits not only in terms of sustainability but also when it comes to other aspects of community resilience. Investing in assets allows communities to own their productive activity together, stewarding resources for future generations. Installing community-owned renewable energy infrastructure (e.g. constructing and running solar, wind and geothermal systems) reduces reliance on fossil fuels and lowers emissions while also creating new jobs and stimulating economic development and local self-sufficiency. The financial benefits of power generation and energy supply return to our communities, in contrast to the systemic inequality of power companies making record profits from their polluting activities. Retrofitting homes and buildings – installing insulation, sealing air leaks, upgrading heating and cooling systems – saves money on energy bills. In short, community climate action can generate profit with a purpose.

Central to our own local proposal, therefore, is that economic activity to deliver value in areas such as retrofitting homes should be delivered by a community benefit society. The government offers retrofitting grants, and there is a massive market opportunity for retrofitters to meet their legislative targets by 2035. Private companies are set to profit from this, but we propose setting up our own company to deliver this work, directing profits back into the community at the same time as training our young people for a green transition into jobs that suit the future we are heading for. (We are working with our anchor institutions, such as West Suffolk College, Suffolk University and the University of East Anglia, to put on courses to meet these needs.) The local system change we want to create is based around co-ops as an economic model: a genuine green transition with democratically controlled assets, and with any surplus accruing to the benefit of the community.

The economic viability of green activities also helps us imagine different models for funding infrastructure through investment. Projects like ours are too small for pension funds to invest in directly, but both parish councils and county councils have the power to borrow significant amounts of money from investment funds, in the form of municipal investment bonds, to support local infrastructure development. Councils underwrite the investment, derisking the bonds and allowing big investment funds to 'green' their portfolios – an attractive proposition for all, and one that allows us to think realistically about large capital investment in green infrastructure. The eternal question of where the money is coming from doesn't have to stall local ambitions so long as we have the imagination to see beyond the current structures of profit and power and dare to build something that works differently.

Community regeneration

It's not all about large-scale planning and infrastructure. There is a vital role for communities to play in areas such as increasing biodiversity and restoring natural habitats. Across the country, citizens have begun reclaiming corners of local land, planting trees and vegetation, creating backyard habitats and kerbside gardens, growing food. This work regenerates communities inside *and* out, not only restoring habitat but rebuilding bonds of trust and friendship through collaborative efforts to nurture our shared environment. Wherever these things are happening, people are learning ways of living in better relationship with each other and the land that supports us.

These on-the-ground measures sit naturally alongside ongoing work to educate our communities about climate change and the importance of taking action. Community groups host workshops and events, provide resources and information, and work with schools and other community organizations to raise awareness. By raising the profile of climate action, communities can inspire others to act and create a ripple effect of positive change. Meanwhile, local networks are strengthened in common cause. And awareness raising is not confined to local citizens: some communities are lobbying local, county and national governments to adopt policies that reduce emissions and support renewable energy development.

Cultivating conditions

Relationship is the cornerstone of community climate action: getting outside our artificial, individual bubbles and starting to have conversations. Before we can start collaborating, we need to do a little patching back together of our social fabric – and then, once we are together, collaborating, that weave will become stronger. That is what makes physical space so important: when it comes to relating across political divides, practical experience has taught us that the most important thing is actually gathering people together. Once people meet each other as whole human beings, they are willing – eager, even – to focus on what we share. The relationships in our community require as much care and cultivation as the practical solutions. In fact, they are inseparable.

This includes potentially difficult relationships with local groups that may feel threatened by the notion of climate action in general; many farmers, for example, face significant disruption through both climate change and its mitigation. Smaller farmers are as much a victim of current systems as everyone else, as they find themselves squeezed between big agriculture and supermarkets. Presented with the right plan, many are ready and able to transition to practices like agroecology and organic farming, ensuring the availability of local food. There is lots of money around for rewilding, which is the approach Natural England are taking, and subsidies are available to increase biodiversity. But to make this a reality we must nurture our relationships with food and farmers. As communities we need to support and uphold them as our VIPs – after all, as the saying goes, you might need your doctor or your lawyer now and again, but you need your farmer three times a day.

Farmers know, perhaps better than any of us, what is happening locally with the climate. They are connected to the land and the seasons, and they can see and feel the changes happening. They are already changing their crop rotation and planting, for example, due to lack of water. As climate impacts affect supplies of the food we import from abroad (e.g. Spain is currently experiencing its worst drought for 1,200 years), we need to consider seriously where our food comes from at a local level. Direct connection with our food and its growers, as part of our communities, is the foundation of change – be it urban, peri-urban or rural.

The farming community here in Suffolk has begun joining Community Climate Action. In my own work, I support farms and farming clusters with sustainable business methodology, because it is no good being sustainable or into agroecology if you can't make a profit. We can reclaim profit from big agriculture and from super-markets as there is money out there – it just needs to be distributed more fairly. Farmers are interested in transitioning but it is a risky and lonely process, so its much safer if you join in a cluster and do it together. Farmers need to know how important they are to us – we need to encourage them rather than pointing the finger and blaming them for ecological issues. They are also at a high risk of suicide, and our district council has a You Are Not Alone programme, of which iFarm is a frontline mental health champion.

Community Climate Action both creates the conditions for good relationships and makes use of existing relationships to create new ones. It has wide appeal because it doesn't scream 'radical' and because it doesn't take the stance of an outsider trying to force a set of values or actions on a community of people. In contrast, it involves local people in the decisions that concern them, helping them create their own plan to build what is needed, where it is needed – based on their own values, in ways that make perfect sense on the ground. We are seeking deep transformation for sure, but we start with what is nearby, relatable and possible. We might borrow the architectural term 'structure-preserving transition' here – in other words, we do not need to tear it all down at once. We can use the tools that we already have at our disposal to build the new structures we want to see.

Local change for global impact

A mass mobilization of civil society is required if we are to meet our emergency targets. The size of the task seems impossibly vast – until you consider the *scalability* of an idea that simply supports local people to create and implement their own achievable goals. By bringing together our residents, stakeholders, volunteers, communities, anchor institutions, faith and religious institutions, local government and cities we can facilitate change house by house, street by street, neighbourhood by neighbourhood. And across the country, groups are already taking action. We find global regenerative communities, community energy groups and installations, and Community Benefit Societies set up to retrofit homes. We see urban and rural movements for organic food production, NGOs acting to protect nature, and a move towards participatory politics, with a People's Plan for Nature.[13] What is now necessary is to amplify and connect this activity, coordinating its action and breaking down the silos we have operated in.

While governments and international organizations still have a critical role to play, communities don't need to ask permission to mitigate damage and protect what they love – or to try to inspire others to do the same. The cumulative impact of citizen action at a local level has untold power to exert pressure on decision makers and help drive change at a larger scale. But perhaps more importantly, we are not waiting for a government that is dragging its heels as the world burns. Starting today, right where we are, we can empower each other to lead the change that we need – and to give a decent answer to the question that future generations are sure to ask: 'What did you do?'

NOTES

1   To paraphrase Noam Chomsky.

2   See https://ozone.unep.org/treaties/vienna-convention.

3   See www.unep.org/ozonaction/who-we-are/about-montreal-protocol.

4   BBC (2013). A brief history of climate change. Science & Environment article (www.bbc.co.uk/news/science-environment-15874560).

5   See www.un.org/en/conferences/environment/rio1992.

6   United Nations (1998). Kyoto Protocol to the United Nations Framework Convention on Climate Change. Report (https://unfccc.int/resource/docs/convkp/kpeng.pdf).

7   Stern, N. (2006). *The Economics of Climate Change: The Stern Review*. London School of Economics.

8   See www.un.org/en/climatechange/paris-agreement.

9   Cuff, M. (2023). Strong El Niño could make 2024 the first year we pass 1.5°C of warming. *New Scientist*, 13 January (www.newscientist.com/article/2354672-strong-el-nino-could-make-2024-the-first-year-we-pass-1-5c-of-warming/).

10   Rannard, G. (2022). Past seven years hottest on record – EU satellite data. BBC Science & Environment article, 10 January (www.bbc.co.uk/news/science-environment-59915690).

11   Public Health England (2019). Public Health England publishes air pollution evidence review. News story, 11 March (www.gov.uk/government/news/public-health-england-publishes-air-pollution-evidence-review).

12 Van der See, B. (2017). UK is 30–40 years away from 'eradication of soil fertility', warns Gove. *The Guardian*, 24 October (www.theguar dian.com/environment/2017/oct/24/uk-30-40-years-away-eradication -soil-fertility-warns-michael-gove).

13 See https://peoplesplanfornature.org/.

CHAPTER 6

Catalysing climate consciousness: moderate rebels connecting heads and hearts

Helena Farstad

Disruptive direct action is an effective way of getting attention, but awareness is incomplete without *dialogue*. XR Catalysers set out to bridge the gap between protesters' demands and the understanding among institutional 'insiders' of what was being asked of them. To carry the message into the corridors of power they set aside disruptive tactics, helping senior decision makers to connect with themselves and others, and to engage emotionally with the crisis – ultimately finding agency on their own terms. Beneath the executives trapped in systems of power and models of success, they met relatable people, distracted from the acuteness of the crisis by business-as-usual but capable of owning their part in upholding a destructive system. By finding ways to instil responsibility without blame, XR Catalysers created untold impact within the sectors that wield real power.

We're walking through the doors opened by our fellow rebels out on the streets, with the intention to connect head and heart, and help people feel the climate and nature breakdown for themselves.
— Roc Sandford, co-founder of XR Catalysers

IMPOSSIBLE IS ONLY A CONSTRUCT OF THE MIND

In summer 2019 London was still coming down after one of the biggest displays of peaceful mass civil disobedience for decades. Extinction Rebellion had brought the capital to a standstill and demonstrated that 'impossible' is simply a construct of the mind. Who, before the bridges were occupied, would ever have imagined a skate ramp on Waterloo Bridge? Or, indeed, trees, tents or a pink boat in the middle of Oxford Circus?

We first met on a hot afternoon in mid summer at Soho House. With quite some trepidation, I found myself sitting around a table with people I hardly knew. There was Caroline Pakel, Roc Sandford, Adam Woodhall and me. I had met Adam once during planning for the October Rebellion, and I had met Roc twice: first on one of the bridges in April that year and then again at a party.

During that party, Roc and I had discussed the need in activism for dialogue, openness and engagement within the existing system, and about the opportunity to create relationships with people of influence and power in order to move the dial and accelerate the decarbonization of the UK economy. Roc called me days later and asked if I would be interested in meeting others in XR who felt the same way. I was. However, as I quickly realized, the prospect of engaging with C-suite leaders in companies that were the main culprits of the environmental crisis had to be approached with care. What would the wider movement think if they knew a group of rebels were engaging in deep conversation with leaders of oil and gas companies or insurance and financial institutions? Was it impossible?

INTERNAL DISRUPTION VERSUS NON-VIOLENT DIRECT ACTION

XR Catalysers, formed by Caroline and Roc, came about because a gap was identified between the demands made on the streets by the rebels, and the people inside the institutions of power, who didn't necessarily understand what was needed of them. Indeed, without clear and relevant demands, the ease with which 'othering' could

become a strategy for executives to deepen denial and resist significant change was a real risk, and one that could increase in line with
the intensity of the protests. When reaching out to people as high up
in organizations as possible, we always promised to leave all disruptive protest tactics at the door (e.g. we would not glue ourselves to
anything); and when we stepped into the offices of the decision makers, we didn't bombard them with facts and figures but instead tried
to help them to relate to the mass outcry, grief, fear and desperation
that had brought thousands to the streets demanding a response to
the failure to act on climate change. To start this process, we needed
to understand the industry, the language, the challenges and the
barriers that were stopping individuals and organizations taking the
necessary steps toward change at the necessary speed.

Our approach was twofold.

(1) To educate ourselves on the key sectors that make up the
    ecosystem of our economy, e.g. the insurance industry, the
    accountants, the asset managers and financial institutions, the
    consultants and advisors, and (perhaps most risky of all) the oil
    and gas companies themselves and the governmental institu-
    tions that are much influenced (and perhaps even controlled)
    by them.

(2) To create tools for connecting people of influence and power
    with themselves, with others and ultimately with the environ-
    mental crisis. Also, to find ways to help those influential people
    'feel' the emergency and their role within it, and to call for
    them to step up and act with agency within their own spheres
    of reach.

We thus went about actively recruiting people that were supportive
of the cause but not ready to take to the street, asking them to meet with
us and tell us everything about their industries. We wanted to know
how things worked, where the weak points were, what they perhaps
themselves wanted to say but did not feel capable of saying – and then
we wanted an introduction to the most senior levels of the organization
or institution. While many did not want to be seen with or associated

with XR publicly, there was, for most, too much excitement (albeit mixed with trepidation) to meet with us to turn down our request to see who these 'rebels' were. We sometimes met via Zoom, sometimes at their offices and sometimes in more secretive places. We were always clear we would not cause physical disturbance, but we did explain that our intent was for internal disruption, connecting their cognitive understanding of the crisis with their emotional understanding and inviting them to feel what was going on. By piercing their denial and helping them relate in a personal way – and by connecting the dots and giving them the space to understand that their families, too, were in danger as a result of the environmental crisis – our theory was that this internal shift could create real impact due to their relative power and levels of influence within the system.

MEETING AS PEOPLE

We agreed not to talk about who we met, and not to publicly share names with either the movement or the press. Our intent was never to expose, never to disrespect, never to blame. We did, however, always invite our counterparts to be guided by the XR meeting 'protocol': to check in and meet as people, carefully facilitated in order to remove power structures and impose equality. This could be a challenging and even painful experience for those who, due to their status, were used to controlling their surroundings, but it was essential to ensure equal share of voice. We always made a point of starting and ending on time, and I believe the hundreds of meetings we had during the 2019–2021 period provided not only significant and thought-provoking conversation but also a realization that things can be done differently: in a more egalitarian, more collaborative, more personable and (certainly to many people's surprise) more effective way.

Being able to speak absolutely freely, adopting the language of the industry, being sympathetic of the challenges and the complexities and yet taking an entirely uncompromising stance, I would dare to suggest that we moved many to connect with what was going on outside on the street. We were not opponents, or indeed even very different from those we met, despite their expensive suits, high-flying careers and secure financial situation. The main difference was 'just' our laser focus on the acuteness of the matter at hand, which can so easily get distorted as part of operational process, organizational noise, financial profiteering and own personal ideas of 'success'. We brought the urgency back into the room and we found ourselves united in wanting a future for our children, and for their children, and for their children's children, and for people elsewhere in the world who were already being terribly harmed by the climate crisis.

Despite being financially very comfortable, the people we met were in some ways also a kind of victim: trapped in the system, feeling unable to break free. Could we share with them a different way of being and help them respond to the climate and ecological crisis?

The ongoing work of XR Catalysers is currently focused on the energy system in particular and, among other things, on how to support such 'change makers' working the system from the inside. In our experience, applying internally obtained intelligence, through external and targeted pressure, is very effective, and this was always the core basis of our theory of change. However, it is still not enough.

CHANGE FROM WITHIN THE SYSTEM

A founding principle of the work of XR Catalysers is that change at the rate we need has to come from people with their hands on the levers of power, and it is our objective to help initiate this change. Following up from initial meetings, we invited our connections to attend 'fire circles'. As Caroline often put it: 'For thousands of years people have been sitting around the fire, sharing stories, problems and concerns, listening intensely to each other and sharing deeply from their heart.'

The fire circle – and what was to become a series of circles: fire, earth, water, air – was a key dialogic method in our toolkit, and one that also took us to Davos in January 2020, where we held several fire circles in hotel venues as well as at the Arctic Basecamp there. Davos was, in its own right, an experience that was simply unreal. It was a microcosm of the power structures and the egos that create them, and it was saturated by an anxious energy that made so many of us feel like entirely dispensable and replaceable cogs in a system. I would never want to go back.

It was also during our trip to Davos that I got to meet Rupert Read properly, as he was accompanying us as part of the XR Catalysers cohort. Due to his profile, Rupert was invited to speak at several meetings and dinners, and he helped us cultivate some extremely valuable contacts, some of which the energy group is still working with today.

On the train back to London I felt exhausted and low on hope, but I felt some relief when Mac Macartney, who also accompanied us on our journey, said: 'We must have faith that "the wall" has started to crumble – and we simply do not know right now how many more stones need to be shifted until the whole structure will fall.'

We have held space for hundreds of people in various circles, providing them with the opportunity to step into a space as humans – not as directors, policymakers or professionals, but fully as themselves – and share their personal stories and feelings about environmental collapse, while also listening to others. We have helped them to see what is happening, and what parts we ourselves play in upholding the system that is so destructive.

Two things became particularly clear to me through this work.

- We have forgotten how it feels to share openly and truthfully and to be listened to without judgement. How powerful this can be as a tool for change and transformation was clear.
- We need to embrace our feelings fully and accept the impact of our actions on the natural world, and by consequence on ourselves, if we are to find the courage to stop being part of causing harm.

IN THE SHADOWS OF POWER

Working behind the scenes within the activist movement with our augmented theory of change – to develop clear and deliverable 'asks' of the institutions we were dealing with – was a continuous challenge. As transparency sits at the core of XR, we Catalysers had to leep a low profile in order to be effective while at the same time being entirely visible and accessible. The opposition and mistrust we occasionally had to manage when sharing insight from talking with the 'other side' took a toll. We did not ask for financial support for our work, and we therefore found ourselves periodically running out of energy and resources. We did, however, always share relevant information with the movement (completely anonymized, never disclosing the names of people or organizations) in order to support and influence future protests actions and to help refine demands.

During early 2020 we thus expanded our reach and insight, and the core group expanded to include Ekatarina de Rodzianko and many others who contributed in sub-circles operating within the XR holacratic 'structure'. Our particular areas of coverage were energy, finance, accountancy, consultancy and insurance.

We started organizing ourselves to reflect this ecosystem, creating working circles focusing on the system's different soft spots, meeting regularly and establishing streams of information from external sources to aid protest. Although our main focus was always to influence decision makers directly through emotional shifts and to support them to advocate and drive internal change, our intent was also to provide the wider movement with relevant information and insight into this wider ecosystem so that they focused on the right institutions, refining their demands in ways that were relevant to the ones they were targeting. It did not always go according to plan, but I did witness a few fantastic actions where international banks and insurance companies were exposed in the most creative and impactful ways.

Then, when the first Covid lockdown arrived in March 2020, everything changed, and nothing changed.

XR had organized via Zoom since its inception, so moving online was easy. However, we did wonder how we could apply our fire circle concept, and replicate the closeness created by sitting around a circle in person, in a virtual environment. Intense effort went into the dry run of the first virtual fire circle. To our surprise, not only did it work, it was almost better. Running the circles virtually allowed far more people to attend, from different places in the world and from different backgrounds. Childcare, travel expenses, timezones and so on were less of a barrier. We experimented with sector-specific circles and developed the programme further.

A MORE RADICAL FLANK

In some ways, we represented a *more* radical flank of one of the most radical environmental movements that had arisen in the UK or globally for decades. Combining radical truth telling and confidence to communicate in ways that people needed to hear, and so they could relate to our messages, our aims were wholly uncompromising, but our approach was based on open dialogue, delivered with love and upheld in even the most complex of situations. I would argue that the impact this work had on the individuals we met was indeed very disruptive, and that it had an untold wider impact. I can summarize what our work taught us with three points.

- While tangibly disruptive direct action that can be sensationalized by the media is a very effective way of significantly and rapidly increasing awareness of an issue, there needs to be dialogue between parties alongside that increased awareness. The dialogue is not necessarily in order to seek agreement, but instead to establish interconnectivity between humans and recognize that we are together in this quest.
- We need to support each other in connecting with the crisis at an emotional level. Unless we allow ourselves to truly feel the grief of loss and the fear for the future, and unless we channel this energy into something constructive, it is too easy to simply fall back into business as usual. Without support, the pain can be too great, resulting in either denial or depression and paralysis.
- Regardless of our backgrounds, our professional careers or our socioeconomic situation, there is more that connects us than divides us. However, it is true that some of us are more responsible and have more influence than others. We need to allocate this responsibility without blame, and apply pressure where significant change can take place. Above all, we must continually test and adapt our methods to make sure they are working, and we must be actively working to find better ones.

WE NEED A MAJORITY DEMANDING CHANGE

I am not personally directly involved with the work of XR or XR Catalysers any longer, as it is not where I think I can now have the most impact. I remain supportive of non-violent direct action and of some of the tactics of groups such as XR and Just Stop Oil, and

I believe those groups are still sadly needed – both for individuals, to help them direct their anger, despair, fear, creativity and courage, and also to force the system to sit up and listen. But I do think that when disruptive tactics are used they need to be targeted and intelligent. Additionally, I have come to realize that, even with external protest, influencing people in positions of power is not enough. We also desperately need a way to mobilize on a society-wide scale, where a majority of people demand change. That calls for a complementary XR Catalysers approach: one that is respectful and informed about the people and communities that are being engaged; that speaks in languages that more people can understand; and that demonstrates that we are not 'different' but that we are all in this together. As such, XR Catalysers has already successfully embodied much of the Climate Majority Project's theory of change: a vehicle for collective inner work, where a truthful narrative, delivered in supportive conditions, creates conditions for individual transformation in the values and mindset that underpin behaviour in the world.

The work of XR Catalysers has, I hope, shifted more people than we can possibly imagine. I have witnessed first hand the radical transformation in some of these people, and I can only assume from this that those people are representative of others. For me, not only has our work created invaluable insight, it has also spurred on other movements and activities that are making a real difference right now. And on a personal note, this work left me with lifelong friendships and support networks, without which I would not have been able to remain hopeful while holding the terrible truth of climate and ecological breakdown. For that I will always be grateful.

'Working with Catalysers has been a fantastic experience for me and my team. They've helped us stretch our minds to move from big words to practical actions. I have no hesitation in recommending engagement with the Catalysers team if you too want to move beyond words to practical actions.'
— Andy Woodfield, Global Client Partner, PwC

CHAPTER 7

Local climate hubs: come for solutions, stay for community

Based on the words of Ruth Allen,
Bel Jacobs, Anna Hyde, Ben Macallen
and Carolyn Dare, by Rosie Bell

Climate hubs are a physical home for climate action in local communities. Recognizing the interdependency between the climate emergency and the social crises playing out in daily life, the philosophy behind these community-run spaces is global-localism. A blueprint for distributed response to the wider crisis, rooted in local realities.

Going by several names, local climate hubs or climate emergency centres (CECs) are a co-created initiative that is picking up momentum across the country. Launched by Ruth Allen and John Phoenix, the concept centres around dedicated physical *space*, encouraging local people to transform disused buildings in high-footfall community areas into hubs for collaborative climate action. Within and around these hubs, networks of climate actors coalesce, form supportive relationships and find many ways to build local resilience. Reaching beyond the 'usual suspects' of eco-activism, however, they aim to engage local government, businesses and other community bodies. Thus established, centres also become a much-needed point of entry for climate-concerned citizens who are new to taking action.

While they are strongly solutions focused – several centres set out specifically to foster stakeholder collaboration towards robust local climate action plans – most founders cite a community-oriented motivation for setting up their group, and report that, similarly, their participants often 'come for the solutions but stay for the community'. Seeking a material answer to the question 'What can I do?', citizens are finding new (and old) ways to be with each other, to collaborate in common cause, and to build deep resilience borne of real social connection. Founders tend to agree that success therefore depends on cultivating inclusive, non-threatening spaces.

Launching independently or evolving out of existing local climate projects, hubs propagate largely via word of mouth; taking root in new areas via webs of relationship, and learning as a network. This growth doesn't 'just happen', however: Ruth highlights the importance of fostering connections and relationships and has put immense resources into cultivating the network to interact and build shared identity. An increasingly robust body of crowd-sourced knowledge and resources also supports this effort, demystifying awkward tasks like applying for charitable status and approaching landlords. This gives new teams the confidence to realize their own vision within tested formats. As they create their hub around the needs of their own community, their unique experience generates more 'how-to' resources, which in turn feed back into the network to support others. Every centre takes a different route, but they are commonly found in empty retail units. An open-source handbook contains, among other things, advice for securing use of such properties.[1]

Each self-funding local team is autonomous, and there is no requirement to adhere to any central strategy, although several groups focus on supporting local government to deliver on net zero pledges following councils' climate emergency declarations. This networked autonomy gives the climate hub mycelium its resilience: while organizers often feel empowered by a sense of belonging to something much larger, no one organization steers or takes ownership of identity or activities. The network has a momentum of its own. Its energy is manifested in the locally run hubs, and the shapes they take depend on the unique strengths and experiences of their founders and communities. In the spirit of this model, this chapter introduces hubs via the 'on-the-ground' experience of some local organizers, exploring their vision and motivations, what they have built, and the challenges and insights that have arisen.

'COMMUNITY COHESION AND COLLABORATION' — BEN MACALLAN, ZERO GUILDFORD

Members of the climate hub network speak of ZERO Guildford[2] in reverent tones – its achievements are widely considered a 'benchmark'. Ben Macallan credits this success to several important factors: intelligent framing, preparatory networking, and 'a ton of people putting in a lot of hard work'.

Before considering a premises, or even a core proposition, the founders worked to build their network, reaching out to representatives of many local climate action groups like the Guildford Environmental Forum and Plastic Free Guildford and teaming up with the University of Surrey. Initial scoping helped determine what existing groups wanted and how collaboration might be achieved. The September 2019 climate strikes became a catalyst: several groups joined forces to support the youth strikers and gathered a 1,000-strong crowd (unheard of in the quite-conservative Surrey borough), usefully highlighting the value of working together. Registering as a charity took six months; acquiring a building took another eight. Actually, says Ben, this potentially frustrating delay was a blessing in disguise. The group needed this time to set up robust governance, sort out policy, 'get on top of the boring stuff' and recruit volunteers.

By the time the 'meanwhile lease' was signed on a high street unit that had seen better days, hordes of volunteers were standing by to fix it up. The team set out to create a 'one-stop shop' in which multiple climate organizations could have a permanent presence and raise awareness. It quickly became clear that real engagement would require more of a 'hook': a reason to stop by that actually served local people's priorities. Using reclaimed and donated materials, and their own know-how, the team built a cafe and, using old bookcases from the University of Surrey's sociology department, a zero-waste shop. Supported by a lottery grant, they launched a 'library of things', where people were able to borrow useful equipment. (The assorted elements bring additional layers of complexity, and the group now employs a bookkeeper to stay on top of things.)

Surrey County Council has a climate change delivery plan but, as Ben observes, 'when you break it down, something like 97% of the county's emissions come down to communities needing to do something'. The climate hub rapidly became a significant platform for outreach and collaboration around these challenges. ZERO teamed up with Take the Jump (a charity focused on action to reduce emissions in local communities) and partnered with the University of Surrey to launch the sustainable business network, which supports local businesses (fifty of them, and counting) to build sustainable management plans, via Clean Growth UK's Net Zero 360 course.[3] Drawing on money from the LoCASE (Low Carbon Across the South and East) programme, they are currently able to provide matched funding for business sustainability and decarbonization projects. An 'energy circle' is taking shape, with funding to conduct business energy surveys, and in partnership with Energy Action Redhill and Reigate the group recently trained thirty-five energy champions to conduct free home energy surveys locally, with an aim to develop towards training domestic retrofit assessors. A citizen science water testing programme is set to expand across Surrey this year.

Ben points out the value of attitude research, such as Britain Talks Climate,[4] in building a successful community offering by listening to how people themselves conceive of the issues and shaping solutions around what they actually want. For the same reason, ZERO prefers not to call itself a 'climate emergency centre': research shows that the words 'climate emergency' turn people off when 'the whole point is to build collaborative action across the political spectrum'. Naming the initiative appropriately (or at least not inappropriately) speaks to the core challenge of framing the call to action to enfranchize and empower rather than repel or overwhelm their target audience – which, at this urgent moment, is basically everyone. Despite the hub's impressive material success, the team puts a great deal down to communication: 'How do we actually build messaging around shared values and local concerns?'

ROOTING CLIMATE RESPONSE IN THE LAND — CAROLYN DARE, CLIMATE ACTION TAUNTON & BLACKDOWN HILLS ECO HUB

When she got involved with the CEC network, Carolyn Dare, a behavioural change consultant and professional facilitator, was seeking a sustainable way of reintegrating into her local community after several years working abroad. From their temporary base in a former Topshop building (shared with a local Rotary club), the newly formed Climate Action Taunton focused on taking climate messaging into the community via local markets, literary fairs, public speaking engagements and people's assemblies. Now based in the shared premises of Lesser Litter, a refill and ethical store, volunteers and trustees chat with local people to build awareness as well as organizing regular events.

Carolyn's focus has since expanded to include more direct, land-based action: among the biggest environmental issues directly affecting local communities is soil depletion and run-off. She became secretary of the Blackdown Hills eco group and partnered with Trimplants, a friend's local wholesale nursery, to establish the Blackdown Hills Eco Hub as a land CEC.[5] They began by making their own biochar: pyrolizing brash from hedge cutting that would otherwise have been burned by local farmers to sequester carbon and enrich the microbial environment and general health of soil. Through related workshops including hedgerow medicine, brash gathering and natural wreath making, they gave isolated communities a centre of gravity and established a strong network. Sympathetic voices came out of the woodwork locally: biologists, regenerative farmers, tree and fungal experts, etc. The hub became a platform to support their existing work and allow their voices to be heard.

Exciting research projects, including a partnership with Plymouth University and Low Carbon Devon, have begun to yield very promising evidence for biochar in terms of thermal green wall installations, soil resilience and increased crop yield. This has led to international connection with groups using biochar to support urban tree planting. The unique partnership has generated a diverse network of connections from green hydrogen experts to soil specialists. Caroline is launching a food-growing group to support local food security while also propagating permaculture methods and supporting further biochar research. As well as taking a bottom-up approach to local adaptation, the group aims to bring isolated people together in connection with the land and to restore the sense of community that underpins resilience. None of this activity requires a bricks-and-mortar premises – perhaps a polytunnel for more challenging weather! For this more rurally oriented hub, land itself is the physical locus of regenerative community.

'ENGAGE; INFORM; CONNECT' — BEL JACOBS AND ANNA HYDE, ISLINGTON CLIMATE EMERGENCY CENTRE

Bel Jacbos had been wondering how to scale up local climate action in Islington for some time when she encountered the idea of climate hubs. Formerly active in XR and still firmly supportive of their tactics, she found herself questioning her own role in radical activism as a route to real impact. Despairing of top-down solutions after another disappointing COP, she was attracted to the idea of a physical hub where climate issues could be addressed locally and collaboratively. XR left her with a strong sense of the nourishment people took from coming together in shared expression of grief and desire for action. But Covid lockdowns had left her community more fragmented than ever, with many feeling isolated. Bel's instinct was to get people together again, talking to each other 'not as "activists" … just as ordinary individuals; concerned citizens talking to other concerned citizens'.

Bel's partner in this initiative, Anna Hyde, was a marketing director in media with a history of organizing as part of the People's Vote campaign. A primary school governor and the mother of a climate-concerned child, her first action in the climate space was to initiate a series of primary school protests (including thirteen schools at their peak) attended by members of parliament, the borough's mayor and national media and contributing directly to a 2030 net zero commitment from the local council. As Anna says: 'Hands down, the best way to cut across any social divide is primary school children.'

Anna quickly found herself up to her neck in the media end of XR, and she organized a number of high-profile events before becoming frustrated by how easy the organization had become to vilify: 'too middle class; too crusty'. Seeking another way to reach across a perceived social divide (and deeply inspired by Ben and Stephanie at ZERO Guildford) after a brief stint working towards the Climate and Ecological Emergency Bill, she teamed up with Bel to launch Islington Climate Centre:[6] to engage a broader spectrum of people on climate but also because 'when the shit hits the fan, community, collectivism is really important; building stuff from the bottom up is going to be really important'.

With the existing handbook as a template ('it's really brilliant that it's just out there for people to grab hold of'), Bel and Anna held a panel discussion to propose the idea to their community and to local decision makers, including borough councillors and members of the Green Party. Finding local landlords and estate agents hard to engage directly, Bel eventually met the owner of a former burger restaurant in the Angel Central arcade at another NGO's event in the space. After a first casual pitch of the idea was dismissed as 'incomplete and unprofessional', the pair created an impressive set of resources, including a designed visual identity and a fully articulated pitch presentation. Following their successful pitch they were offered rent-free use of the space and they added their template to the pool of resources available to other fledgeling climate hub initiatives.

The group found that their retail centre suited their aims perfectly. While perhaps counterintuitive to a purist's vision of climate action, a Central London space where people were popping in with their shopping bags felt like exactly the right place to 'meet people where they are'. Plans evolved as the organizers learned by doing, with evening events proving more practical than hosting a drop-in space for busy shoppers. An imagined schedule of weekly, themed sustainability fairs pulling together local climate groups gave way to more manageable, targeted activities in which participants could engage deeply with a specific issue. Teaming up with groups such as Hackney and Shoreditch Greenpeace, they hosted film screenings and exhibitions; and mending and repair workshops for technology and garments. There were grief circles and talks about insulation, vegan bake-sales and toy-swapping. A North London COP 'climate festival' was attended by press. Most successful of all have been weekly events that have a growing following. Climate Fresk, a card game that teaches players a systemic view of the climate and ecological crisis, has become hugely popular.

Thanks to a somewhat elusive volunteer base, a drop-in model has been hard to establish. Despite strong interest and sign-up, the centre has been carried for the most part by its two committed founders, absorbing immense time and personal resources in the process. It's not clear why the group struggles to galvanize a regular commitment from volunteers. Is it a symptom of London's busyness? Bel wonders whether future collaborations could aim beyond the sphere of explicit climate action. Can local community centres be recruited to the kind of juicy, generative climate work that serves both citizen empowerment and planetary health?

At events themselves, however, community reception has been overwhelmingly warm, highlighting to the founders the importance of giving people somewhere to go. Post-Covid, Anna notes, the people turning up 'fresh' without prior engagement in climate networks were often those who had been alone during lockdown: those 'who just wanted a chat and a hug, and a hangout'. Both founders feel that the project's great value has been in facilitating community.

A WEB OF INTERDEPENDENCIES

Individually and as a network, local hubs demonstrate the climate action that resists neat categories. Here is a genuine ecosystem: messy, fractal, generative. The founders, many activated by radical circles, have found their own work to do in mainstream territory, and most straddle numerous other projects. Participant demographics range from activists and groups using a platform to meet and swap stories, tactics and social technologies, to concerned citizens, newly awake to the crisis. If a single factor unites them, it is an effort to meet everyone where they are and to support them to move along a spectrum of engagement, channelling growing climate concern into awareness raising, network building and practical empowerment. Much of this work bears fruit elsewhere: those who engage at the centre take home seeds of change that are propagated throughout life. For this reason it can be difficult for those involved to gauge impact, but no initiative that aims at system change can hope to measure its success in the short term. At a strategic level, founders regularly emphasize the long-term interdependence of top-down and bottom-up action. In the absence of adequate global leadership, communities are beginning to take adaptation and resilience into their own hands – while helping to build legitimacy for high-level policy change.

WHERE NEXT?

Many climate hubs are still in an early phase of life and founders each have their own vision for how they would like to see their centres evolve.

While honouring the hub as a space for grassroots action, Liz Day and Jenny Haycocks from Gathering Gates Norfolk see place as a means to longer-term system and culture change – from inquiry into collective intelligence and group process to just distribution of power: 'How do we walk this path to a better world in such a way that we really demonstrate the change we want to see?'

Others are relieved to have found an action-forward space and are bursting with ideas for manifest energy: 'A co-working space, a kilo shop, a cafe … you know, and just kind of have a vibe, because that's how people meet each other.' Anna Hyde hopes to see the Islington project evolve into regular people's assemblies: accessible spaces for real deliberation, properly linked via press contacts to local spheres of influence. Modelling bottom-up democracy while demonstrating a local mandate for top-down change.

Elsewhere, organizers call for strengthening the global CEC 'commons of knowledge', for centralized fundraising and for more support in sourcing venues. While a decentralized model brings flexibility and resilience at a network level, there is a sense that the DIY format too easily becomes a recipe for burnout for a committed core of individuals. Sustainability remains a challenge for teams.

As centres proliferate (there are more than forty at the time of writing) they continue to evolve, cross-pollinating ideas and strengthening their substrate networks of existing grassroots climate organizers. Their story is naturally unfinished, and readers are warmly invited to continue it. If you are interested in finding out more about climate hubs, the open-source handbook now lives at https://cecnetwork.org. The Taunton and Guildford hubs (carolyn. dare@gmail.com and info@zerocarbonguildford.org, respectively), are also happy to guide and connect you.

COME FIND US

With thanks to Anna Hyde and Bel Jacobs (Islington Climate Centre), Ben Macallan (ZERO Guildford), Carolyn Dare (Climate Action Taunton & Blackdown Hills Eco Hub), Charlotte Haigh (Kingston Hive), Climate Hub Bath, Climate Resilience Centre Worthing (CREW), Dorking Climate Emergency, Emma Mary Gathergood (Malvern Green Space), Exeter Community Alliance, Jem Friar (Totnes Climate Hub), Lewes Climate Hub, Liz Day and Jenny Haycocks (Gathering Gates Norfolk), One Planet Abingdon, Oswestry CEC Community Hub, Rachel Bailey, Ruth Allen, Selma Heimedinger (Portsmouth Climate Emergency Centre), Suzanne O'Donnell (Climate Hub Wandsworth), and What Next Godalming.

NOTES

1   See https://cecnetwork.org.
2   See https://www.zerocarbonguildford.org/
3   See https://www.clean-growth.uk/net-zero-360/
4   See https://climateoutreach.org/reports/britain-talks-climate/.
5   See https://cagdevon.org.uk/impact/carolyn-blackdowns-ecohub-transition-group/
6   See https://www.islingtonclimatecentre.co.uk/

Playing the Wild Card: citizens are challenging landowners to restore nature in the UK – starting at the top

Joel Scott-Halkes

In a self-declared nation of nature lovers, how did UK biodiversity end up among the world's most damaged? Grassroots pressure group Wild Card set out to erase the false distinction between our climate and ecological crises, and to press landowners who control vast swathes of the UK countryside – starting with the Crown Estate – into restoring its lost natural wealth. In contrast to the fear-driven messaging that can deter some citizens from climate organizing, the rewilding movement offers a sense of regenerative hope to many. It is a joyful campaign to bring the land back to life.

I have created more than a little disruption in my time. As a national coordinator in XR's action circle, I helped organize acts of civil disobedience that shut down Central London, blockaded coal mines, closed airports, paralysed printing presses, caused howls of outrage from the right-wing billionaire press (although, what doesn't?) and resulted in thousands of arrests.

In a personal capacity I have experienced no shortage of mad situations. I have had my house raided by police, I have had a rib broken by a riot officer, and I once even ended up superglued to the inner thigh of an officer's trousers as he pulled my hand away from a boarding pass scanner in City Airport. Suffice to say, my activism has not always gone to plan.

But recently, I have also tried something radically old fashioned – indeed, about as old fashioned as the history of British protest itself: petitioning the royal family. This might sound like a somewhat mediaeval approach in the midst of the very contemporary and pressing climate crisis, but this experiment has yielded such surprisingly positive results – garnering huge press coverage around the world and forcing action from one of the grandest institutions in the country – that it has left me reflecting on the very nature of the climate movement and the direction it needs to take. Here is the story of a surprising new rewilding movement. Here is the story of Wild Card.

*

At the beginning of lockdown, XR froze. You could not have designed a better immobilizer for a movement based on mass gatherings and mass arrest. I was itching to get people back out on the streets, but ultimately we had to accept that a pause was inevitable. So, like many others who were privileged *not* to be facing danger on the frontlines of the pandemic, I sat at home and read.

It was in the dusty armchair of a Hackney house-sit that I encountered rewilding for the first time. Ironically, for something so real, so outdoorsy and so messy, my journey into the heart of the rewilding movement began at a time when we were only allowed outdoors once a day.

But as I read works like *Feral* by George Monbiot, *Wilding* by Isabella Tree and (later) *Rewilding* by Paul Jepson and Cain Blythe, my imagination exploded. I learned that an intact Britain would naturally feature vast swathes of rare temperate rainforest full of lichens, lynx and pine martens. I discovered that elk, bison and bears once roamed these islands. And most exciting of all, I found that a small but growing movement of people is working to bring our decimated landscapes back to life. As if in answer to the fear, the apocalypticism and the millenarianism of my feelings when I organized XR protests, when I read of beaver reintroductions, rainforest regeneration or the release of white cranes I found the hope I desperately needed.

Rewilding, as I was quickly coming to understand, is the ultimate solution to the trifecta crises of climate, biodiversity and animal exploitation that are destroying our planet today. It is the perfect win–win–win. Evidence shows that changing land use from animal grazing to rewilding could suck down vast amounts of atmospheric carbon – so much so that it could even reverse global heating[1] – while restoring lost habitats and saving plummeting wildlife populations. Every small patch of rewilded land could also shrink the cruel animal agriculture industry, which is responsible for more emissions than the entire global transport sector,[2] while paying farmers to be stewards of a richer natural landscape.

We need rewilding more in Britain than almost anywhere else in the world. Despite being an island of nature lovers, we seem to have cheerily obliterated the more-than-human life of this country more successfully than almost any other nation. When the Royal Society for the Protection of Birds (RSPB) and the Natural History Museum ranked the world's nations for intactness of biodiversity, the UK ranked a shocking 229th out of 240 countries: bottom of the G7 and in the worst 10% globally.[3]

Meanwhile, our tree coverage is dire. Compared with a European average of 38%, Britain has just 13%[4] and England stands at only 10%.[5] But even those figures are misleading, since they represent largely monocultural commercial forestry. The RSPB measures areas actually set aside for nature at just 5%.[6]

This shameful state of affairs flies in the face of the UN's call for 30% of global land and seas to be protected by 2030. But importantly, it also contradicts a very genuine will to protect wildlife that rests in the hearts of the British people. We identify as a nation of nature lovers. But the 'nature' many of us seek to preserve is often a landscape denuded of biodiversity by the agricultural practices of centuries. Sadly, the reason our hearts still sing at the sight of open fields is because we so rarely witness nature that is actually unspoiled.

From this angle, the climate movement, obsessed with the industrial mechanics of emissions and fossil fuels, began to seem like a rather one-dimensional human survival club – a crucial cause, but one that lacked consideration of the 8.7 million other species we share our planet with. And furthermore, it felt like a movement that was likely to fail on such terms anyway without the massive carbon drawdown rewilding could contribute.

As lockdown thawed and I reentered the world, I found that both the UK's physical landscape and the campaigning landscape of the climate movement looked radically different to me. Where once I saw Constable-esque idyll, I was confronted by 'sheepwrecked' deserts, empty of wildlife. And where once I considered climate and the risk of human extinction as the core ideas of the modern environmental cause, I now saw rewilding and a fundamental redefinition of our relationship with non-human life as the priority of any meaningful movement.

But before I could face the intimidating question of how to start a pro-rewilding movement, I felt compelled to ask how we let this happen. Membership of the UK's nature charities is far bigger than the membership of all our political parties combined, yet we have allowed our wild spaces to be decimated. How?

A meeting with the brilliant and tenacious writer-activist Guy Shrubsole gave me the answer: land ownership. Or to be precise, the astonishingly unequal, arbitrary and unjust control of our land by a tiny, wealthy and unaccountable minority.

As Guy's fascinating book *Who Owns England?* discusses, 50% of England's land is currently owned by considerably less than 1% of its population. In Scotland the situation is even more extreme, with half the nation's land owned by fewer than 500 individuals. The aristocracy – a tiny club of around 2,000 – owns 20% of English land, while a third of black families do not even have access to a garden. And among this hidden elite of wealthy landowners are some major household names. Billionaire James Dyson owns 33,000 acres: an area of land bigger than Manchester. The Church of England and the Oxbridge Colleges own 105,000 acres and 126,000 acres, respectively. Most shocking of all, the British royal family owns a mind-boggling 850,000 acres of land and foreshore: an area of land twice the size of Greater London.

Even as these figures set my head spinning, an obvious new campaign target crystallized in my mind. If we are to rewild our land and bring nature back to these islands, we need to take on the landowners.

*

From XR's network, a small band of rewilding rebels quickly took root. After some seriously intense lockdown Zoom conversations with co-founders Clarice Holt and Max Trevitt, a core team formed, including the wonderful Emma Smart, Hazel Draper, Annie Randall, Dr Alison Green, Professor James Bullock, Iris May Phillips and Isobel Hadfield. Our mission was simple: to campaign, by any effective means, to force the UK's biggest landowners to rewild their land.

We knew that if we wanted to speak to landowners, we needed an entirely new identity. Unlike XR, who found themselves pigeonholed by the establishment and the billionaire press as a dangerous bunch of far-left radicals, Wild Card needed to appeal to a true cross-section of society. Our theory, based largely on a strong hunch, was that rewilding appealed as much to conservative *Daily Express* readers as it did to the '*Guardian*-reading tofu-eating wokerati'.[7]

For the campaign's visual and messaging identity our talented designer Clarice summoned the language of heraldry, medievalism and folk tales. In petitioning landowners for their help we were following in the footsteps of peasants from a bygone age, so we decided to evoke a long-lost world in which society still believed in a sense of mutual responsibility between rich and poor. Indeed, as we learned about land inequality it became clear that feudalism is still very much alive in the UK today. The resulting campaign identity was bright and bold, medieval and colourful. It channelled the voice of the court joker: that disruptive but joyful truth teller that a monarch simply cannot bear, but also can't live without.

To a group of revolutionaries united in a fierce desire for system change and brought together by XR, the idea of doffing our caps to the precipitous wealth of landowners did not come easily. As Simon Fairlie and others have pointed out, why stop at rewilding when we ought to be demanding redistribution of land full stop? Pragmatism and the particular urgency of the climate crisis precluded such ambitions in the short term, but we theorized that a large public rewilding campaign had the potential to raise awareness of land issues more generally. Our campaign could help build political consensus towards middle-ground land reform solutions like community right-to-buy, stronger (land) property taxes and the taxing of second homes.

So now for the campaign itself. The royal family was an obvious first campaign target. Not only are they the biggest landowning family in the country, but their totemic international significance meant that calling on them to rewild would help the idea resonate around the world. Furthermore, we had recently discovered that the royals were guilty of some gobsmacking green hypocrisy. Despite their welcome environmental advocacy, the royals' landholdings are in a dreadful state when it comes to nature. The Duchy of Cornwall, for example, which has been owned by Prince (now King) Charles for the last half a century and which was recently inherited by Prince William, includes the biggest single portion of Dartmoor, most of the Scilly Isles, and swathes of high-quality farmland throughout the West Country. Much of this land would naturally be covered in rare temperate rainforest, but take a walk around Dartmoor today and you will find it to be a blasted dead zone, devoid of almost all life. Its tree coverage stands at a shockingly low 5%.

This is not the royal estates' only disaster zone. Balmoral, situated in the Cairngorms National Park, is almost entirely dedicated to bloodsports, leading to problems of overgrazing and the destructive practice of 'muirburn': burning the moors to help create ideal breeding conditions for grouse. In supporting a practice that *literally sets fire* to wild landscapes in the name of sport, we could not help but feel that Prince Charles was failing to live up to his environmental credentials.

From our point of view, however, this high-profile hypocrisy made a great story. By taking the world stage to preach about saving nature while allowing it to be incinerated in their own backyard, the royals had created their own poor optics. We did not need to block any roads – we just had to point out their double standard.

*

First we assembled the big guns. We wrote an open letter to the royals and gathered famous signatories. British TV personalities

Chris Packham, Hugh Fearnley-Whittingstall, Kate Humble and Anita Rani, bestselling author Michael Morpugo and former Archbishop of Canterbury Rowan Williams, among many others, all signed our letter, and we are immensely grateful for their generous support. Next we sought out revered climate scientists. Thanks to the tireless work of Dr Alison Green, we soon added the voices of Sir Bob Watson, former chair of the IPCC, and Sir David King and Sir Ian Boyd, both former Government Chief Scientific Advisors. The letter was eventually delivered with more than 100 signatures, leading to coverage in the mainstream press. Our campaign had begun.

Now it was time for us peasants to gather our kin. We turned to precisely the campaign tactic that I had regularly maligned as pointlessly reformist during my time in XR: a petition. In conjunction with the campaign group 38 Degrees we threw ourselves into gathering signatures. Wild Card activists Emma Smart, Annie Randall and Hazel Draper worked flat out building our network and using social media to achieve this, and 38 Degrees activist Matt Richards was spectacular at mobilizing their base. Amazingly, we reached more than 100,000 signatures.

Next it was time to confront the royals. We needed an emotional strategy. Yes, our campaign made perfect rational and scientific sense, but reason doesn't get you headlines. We needed advocates, and given the royals' (albeit ceremonial) position of responsibility, we knew that young voices were best placed to ask these perennial patrons to save their future.

Two incredible youth-led activist groups arrived at just the right moment. XR Families and the SOS from the Kids choir joined us, along with the indefatigable public treasure that is Chris Packham, to march on Buckingham Palace. Carrying colourful banners and papier mâché animals and singing songs outside the palace, we called on the royals to rewild.

We knew that the impact we wanted would require a media whirlwind. Annie, Clarice and I worked for weeks repeatedly emailing, calling and WhatsApping every journalist we could find contact details for. For a couple of weeks it looked like nobody would turn up, but eventually the invaluable guidance of activist PR guru Ronan

McNern paid off. Every major broadcaster and newspaper in the UK sent a reporter to the front gates of Buckingham Palace. There were so many cameras and reporters there as the children sang that it was as if the real paparazzi had shown up.

Finally, it was time for the ultimate piece of storytelling. The palace initially refused to let us through the gates to hand deliver the petition to the household staff – until I politely reminded them that the world's media were about to see a group of children standing outside closed gates, crying about being turned away. As our emissary to hand over the petition we chose fourteen-year-old Simeon, a founding member of the SOS from the Kids choir. *Now* we (and most of the UK media) had a story. Would the big, rich, powerful and elite royals really say no to a group of schoolchildren asking for their future to be saved?

Thanks to the campaign we received a formal letter from the late Queen's private secretary telling us that the Queen would consider our petition. An insider source revealed that the campaign was discussed at length at 'all levels' of the royal household, and our polling showed that we swung public opinion in favour of our campaign by eleven percentage points. As well as making headline TV news on every UK channel, Wild Card was covered internationally from Canada to France to Pakistan. Additionally, vindicating the theory that rewilding is a truly cross-political issue, the campaign received genuinely positive newspaper coverage from across the spectrum: from the right-wing *Daily Mail* to the left-wing *Mirror*.

But most importantly, we secured a series of high-level meetings with the Crown Estate: the largest of the royal landholdings. These meetings, thanks in no small part to the respectful and joyful tone of our campaign, have been truly productive and collaborative. While we are currently sworn to secrecy as a condition of ongoing dialogue, I can say this much: a significant act of nature restoration from the Crown Estates is now closer than ever. Following the death of the Queen, we are about to launch a whole new chapter of the campaign by calling for the Duchy of Cornwall's new owner, Prince William, to step up and bring back Dartmoor's rainforests.

*

So what does this experiment in peasantish petitioning tell us?

Let us first note what it *does not* tell us. It does not in any way undermine the continuing need for disruptive protest. I am convinced that one reason our campaign succeeded without disruption is because landowners, unlike the government, are not already immune to protest. The bar to gaining attention is therefore lower. Also, importantly, Wild Card is *very* small. In no way can our campaign be compared to, or seen as a successor to, a history-making mass movement such as XR.

What we did learn is this. We found a way of punching way above our weight, in a manner that appealed to many 'moderates'. We discovered that the infectious joy of rewilding is an enormous, cross-political mobilizer. I believe this is because, at a deep level, we all know that we are interconnected with our non-human relatives. Our biophilia and thus our love of rewilding transcends politics and can be a powerful motivator. The climate movement can harness the public's clear desire for a story that goes above and beyond that of human survival versus total apocalypse.

But from a strategic point of view we learned, crucially, that emotion, storytelling and choosing the right messenger can be as powerful as disruption. I therefore ask your permission to end with some reflections on the strategic implications of our experience for the climate movement's ever-evolving theory of change.

When I joined a fledgling XR, my friend Roger Hallam – the movement builder and theorist – told me that the objective was to block the roads until 'Pret A Manger ran out of salad cream'. I was rapt. Essentially, he meant that only when an unbearable level of material disruption was achieved – when big companies and the state were beginning to suffer real financial losses – would you provoke a crisis response from the government.

April 2019's 'pink boat' rebellion, which I proudly helped organize, seemed to prove this theory of change. But since then, the state has proved remarkably resilient to the effects of any such disruption. Insulate Britain and Just Stop Oil have achieved some impressive traffic jams, but they have yet to provoke a COBRA meeting. Meanwhile, in terms of the numbers of people involved, participation in climate protest has dropped considerably since 2019.

The moments that *have* cut through from groups like Just Stop Oil and Animal Rebellion have instead been moments of visual and storytelling brilliance. Throwing soup at a Van Gogh painting, pouring milk on the floor of Harrods, going on hunger strike: these actions won huge media attention and rattled the state, not through particularly severe material or financial disruption but through emotional and psychological disruption. They functioned as story-memes that competed for the public's fractured attention span in the New Media Economy and won.

Does this mean we *cannot* force the state into transformative action with coercive material disruption? Not necessarily. It may, I hope, still be possible. But what it does suggest is that, as every labour strike leader knows, disruption is useless without first winning in the battle ground of narrative and emotion.

It is the emotional force and magic of our stories that will determine the success of our activism, not the reductive logic of material disruption alone. With Wild Card, we found that a story of hope – a story that says humanity *can* undo the harm we caused and bring our beautiful planet back to life – is a story that the public is ready to march for.

NOTES

1   Eisen, M. B., and Brown, P. O. (2022). Rapid global phaseout of animal agriculture has the potential to stabilize greenhouse gas levels for 30 years and offset 68 percent of CO_2 emissions this century. PLOS Climate, 1 February (https://doi.org/10.1371/journal.pclm.0000010).

2   Twine, R. (2021). Emissions from animal agriculture – 16.5% is the new minimum figure. *Sustainability* 13(11):6276 (https://doi.org/10.3390/su13116276). Ritchie, H., Roser, M., and Rosado, P. (2020). CO_2 and greenhouse gas emissions. OurWorldInData.org (https://ourworldindata.org/co2-and-greenhouse-gas-emissions).

3   RSPB (2021). New report shows the UK is the least effective G7 member at protecting nature. Report, 13 May (www.rspb.org.uk/about-the-rspb/about-us/media-centre/press-releases/new-report-shows-the-uk-is-the-least-effective-g7-member-at-protecting-nature/).

4   Forest Research (2018). Forest cover: international comparisons. Tools and Resources (www.forestresearch.gov.uk/tools-and-resources/statisti cs/forestry-statistics/forestry-statistics-2018/international-forestry-3/fo rest-cover-international-comparisons/).
5   Friends of the Earth (2020). England's 10 biggest landowners must grow more trees. Press Release, 4 August (https://friendsoftheearth. uk/nature/englands-10-biggest-landowners-must-grow-more-trees).
6   RSPB (2021). UK failing to protect land for nature. Press Release, 2 September (www.rspb.org.uk/about-the-rspb/about-us/media-centre/ press-releases/uk-failing-to-protect-land-for-nature/).
7   Brown, F. (2022). Home Secretary Suella Braverman blames protest disruption on 'tofu-eating wokerati'. Sky News, 18 October (https:// news.sky.com/story/home-secretary-suella-braverman-blames-protest-disruption-on-tofu-eating-wokerati-12724058).

CHAPTER 9

MP Watch: empowering the citizen

Jessica Townsend

A culture of consumerism is deeply implicated in the climate and ecological emergency, and it also warps our representative democracy and displaces our citizenship in ways that undermine climate action at all levels. Among a number of emerging initiatives focused on reviving democracy, MP Watch aims to reawaken a sense of self as citizen in local communities, supporting constituents to hold their representatives to account as 'the last climate election' approaches.

When I was at school, there was a lesson called citizenship that some progressive schools tried to substitute in for religious education. At my girls' high school, at least, it was deadly dull: uninspiringly taught by a dumped-on teacher from a different specialism. I skipped it as much as I could.

But back in the mid 1970s, British people pretty much took a sense of duty for granted: parents turned up to meet teachers and attended the school concert; families still ate together in the evening around a table; policemen were recognized on their beats; small children were 'seen and not heard'. There were accepted standards of behaviour that I – a credulous, mildly sanctimonious kid – assumed adults adhered to even when no one was looking. All was right with the world. Of course, later – *much* later, actually – I questioned some of these values, realizing, for example, that 'conjugal rights' was more often heard of, back then, than domestic rape.

Yet in one way, the world *was* alright, because in the early 1970s planetary boundaries had not yet been exceeded. Nor was the carbon in the atmosphere yet threatening the stability of the whole biosphere. This was an era when things were less disposable, and while consumerist habits were ramping up, conspicuous consumption was less an integral part of life. Average people rarely took expensive long-haul flights. When they did, it was such an event that they invited all their friends afterwards for an interminable slide show for which no amount of cheese and pineapple on sticks could adequately compensate.

Spin forward through the decades, and individuals today are neither subjects nor citizens, but *consumers*. It takes about twenty years on average for real GDP per capita to double, so in my lifetime that has happened three times. As a nation we are consuming roughly *eight times* more than when I was born. At this rate, by the time I hit eighty that will be sixteen times. A curve that doubles is exponential – the same path that cancer follows – and this means that to keep growth steady, a lot of stuff needs buying, even by those of us with only modest disposable incomes.

So we get cheap credit. We get disposable plastics: spoons, cups and glasses. We get to buy five T-shirts for the price we used to pay for one. We get built-in obsolescence in fridges, phones, computers and cars.

To encourage us not to slacken the pace of our giddy consumer whirl, adverts are beamed at us from every gizmo and public space: by some estimates, people have 6,000–10,000 adverts directed towards them every day.[1] All that content keeps a lot of creatives in work: graphic designers, visual artists, messaging professionals, actors, directors, sound recordists, camera and lighting professionals.

Unsurprisingly, given that deluge of prompting, our neurons are wired for capitalism. How many of you, like me, arrive home exhausted but instead of wanting to sleep instead crave a snack, a drink or a Netflix show, telling ourselves that we deserve it? Then eventually, after a spate of late-night consumption, we tumble into bed to get less sleep than we needed having made another modest contribution towards GDP.

Of course, the formerly slick machinery of growth is beginning to make worrying clanking noises. With cost-of-living and energy crises in full swing, many British people are finding it hard to pay for basic needs, never mind doing their bit to support an exponentially growing economy. It is hard to see how that can continue.

CONSUMER DEMOCRACY

The dominant paradigm of *individual-as-consumer* is not limited to the things we literally buy. We act as consumers of democracy as well. Every four years or so, the main parties put together a manifesto that they market to us. Our role is limited to selecting between these offerings based – as Jon Alexander points out in his book *Citizens* – largely on self-interest.[2]

Any manifesto has a lot of heterogeneous parts, but we are not asked to shape the content, just to pick one. What is more, there is no buyer protection: if the chosen package fails to live up to its promises, there is usually not much we can do besides have a hissy fit on social media, bellyache in little-read newspaper comment sections or moan to our friends in the pub. We can demonstrate on the streets (provided we are not too noisy), but we have to wait another four years or so to demonstrate our frustration by voting for another, minimally different manifesto.

Between elections, politicians and government departments might poll our opinion on various issues, but this secretive process serves their own ends not ours, and results are rarely publicized without a pointed political purpose.

This cyclical model is an ill fit for the complexity of modern life. And unlike our other consumer roles, increasingly disillusioned electorates often decline to participate in the process of actually voting. Perhaps that is unsurprising when ordinary voters are so deprioritized by government, whereas multinational companies, industries and high-wealth individuals – some of whom pay no tax, and certainly at nothing like the rate of a British citizen – can buy influence.

While many decry the state of our democracy, the parties who benefit from that system are the last to react creatively to voter apathy. At the 2021 Labour Party conference a proposal advocating proportional representation was refused, in spite of support from 80% of delegates, by a leadership that felt closer to outright victory than they had for thirteen years.[3]

When it comes to holding power to account, deepening polarization is regularly and ruthlessly deployed as a weapon to derail good-faith dialogue and to prevent change. Meanwhile, market forces feed on the same dynamics to manipulate democracy. In the smartphone era, polarization is deepened by social media algorithms that create profit by learning what content best hijacks our attention (and sense of outrage), hardening our views by serving us ever more of the same. Following her discovery after the Brexit vote that Cambridge Analytica had illicitly harvested 87 million Facebook profiles in order to target users with misleading ads that played on their political fears, the journalist Carole Cadwalladr rightly questioned 'whether it's actually possible to have a free and fair election ever again'. [4] In a world ruled by content marketing, the role of citizen is hostage to the role of consumer.

Manipulation by market interests is likewise written through government (in)action on climate. In spite of the Paris Agreement and the law in place to ensure we meet its requirements, fossil fuel lobbies aggressively push their agenda and block climate policies so that fossil fuel companies can maximize profits before their products become stranded assets.[5] They do this both openly, represented by PR companies, and covertly, disguised as thinktanks: so-called astroturfing. In the UK, the best known of these thinktanks is the Global Warming Policy Foundation, which has been proven by Open Democracy to have taken oil money. Policy Exchange and the Institute of Economic Affairs, both part of the Tufton Street nexus of dark money and secretive lobby groups, have done so too. The nexus also includes government ministers, their special advisers and MPs' networks such as the Net Zero Scrutiny Group, as well as media outlets including GB News, *The Telegraph* and *The Spectator*.

This interference is supported by climate disinformation and greenwashing produced on an industrial scale for international and global audiences. Much of this messaging originates outside our own shores and feeds directly back into our digital consumer culture. The *Deny Deceive Delay* reports from the Institute for Strategic Dialogue and its partners reveal the scale of strategic disinformation surrounding the COP26 and COP27 meetings, showing how social media accounts are used to disseminate and amplify misleading messages and sow confusion.

The UK parliament set up the Committee on Climate Change to look into details of how the country might achieve its Paris 2015 goals. And yet – perhaps unsurprisingly given the forces named above – at a policy level almost nothing has been done. Democracy literally means *rule by the people*, but clearly this is not the nature of our system. Right now, the political system that supposedly responds to the needs of its electorate is not acting to avert an existential threat, despite a dramatic and lasting uptick in public climate concern. The political system is simply not serving us, the demos.

UPGRADING THE SYSTEM?

Fearsome dysfunction in our politics is nothing new, and people have long sought improvements to our democracy, not least the advocates of proportional representation mentioned above. But in the face of institutionalized resistance to electoral reform, innovations are also possible (and necessary) to maximize opportunity for citizen empowerment *within* the current system.

Ireland's use of citizens' assemblies demonstrates the potential for developing instruments to engage the public in decision making. These are based on a selection process known as sortition: a process similar to juror selection to ensure a representative cohort. In stark contrast to the Brexit vote, the Irish Citizens' Assembly brought public opinion together on a highly divisive issue, reaching a durable and popular compromise.

Elsewhere, digital technology supports public consensus generation at scale. One important example is the use of civic tech in Taiwan, where, after a series of clashes, the government responded to the g0v hacks by assimilating their methods into national government practice, appointing the movement's Audrey Tang as a minister to oversee the changes. Now, their VirtualTaiwan digital platform facilitates public deliberation on public matters. For example, in 2015 the government asked how Uber might be regulated to maximize the benefits and minimize the negatives of introducing it in the country. Responders on the platform were invited to first identify their role (driver, passenger, taxi driver, etc.), then state their view and suggest compromises, and then vote on the suggestions of others. Despite fierce divisions at the beginning of the process, 'recommendations emerged that received almost universal approval'.[6]

Because the responders are proposing compromise, the process brings opponents into the middle zone and pulls them closer together – the precise opposite of polarizing forces such as tech interference in the Brexit referendum. We might imagine how such an intervention could help us to establish consensus on any number of important issues: our malfunctioning water companies, for example.

TOWARDS A NEW CITIZENSHIP

No amount of political innovation is sufficient, however, if we, the people, have lost sight of our agency. The democratic edifice ultimately depends on our assent and complicity. If we wanted to, many more of us could try to intervene. Has our confected role of consumer lulled us into passivity? As Rupert Read contests, to call our present system 'consumerist' may be misleading. Mainstream economics propagates a myth that consumer needs are the *pull* factor behind our market economy, when in fact the *push* factor of marketing and advertising is the driving force, *creating* needs that enslave us to the system.[7]

As such we have all but lost sight of how to behave outside of these parameters. We know how to *complain*: that is part of the consumer's toolkit. We can analyse, dissect, debate. But if our complaints are never taken seriously and change nothing at the level of the system, they contribute little more than an illusion of agency.

The first time I was conscious of evading my own role as consumer was when, having read some climate science, I joined a fledgling group called Extinction Rebellion. I remember standing in Oxford Circus, a place most Londoners avoid because of the ceaseless traffic and tourist-crowded pavements, when suddenly, in the middle of the road, there was a pink boat named after Berta Caseres, the murdered Honduran climate activist. On the boat's deck young people spoke of their climate grief. Old people talked about global heating, and at night there were DJs. It was hard to enter the shops nearby; the road was closed.

The temple of consumerism had been transformed, and on waking next morning, those who had spent the night in or around the boat heard something new and strange for those streets: birdsong. We felt we were at the beginning of a transformation that everyone would follow – that we would become a nation of activists and address the climate crisis. Sadly, despite its many achievements, XR never garnered that level of support, and then the pandemic sent us all home, giving enemies of climate action time to regroup. Most people still do not understand the jeopardy we are in, and XR is marginalized. The courage of those risking arrest has been degraded by media hostility. Most people will never embrace the label 'activist'. Nonetheless, within the safer sounding role of 'citizen' there are plenty of ways to empower individuals to take a role in the transformation that is needed.

After all, we are the voters who decide on the government. What if, instead of acting like consumers and choosing something 'off the peg', we tried to engage and influence our politicians and political parties as voters? What if we consistently paid attention, not just to the news, but to what our own MP is doing in our name? What if we asked for meetings with her, inundated her with messages and letters, and discussed our opinions in the local press? What if we engaged personally with the other candidates for an election to try to influence them?

This philosophy of reinvigorating climate action at the constituency level underpins the creation of MP Watch: a grassroots network of local people banding together to hold MPs to account over adequate representation on climate. MP Watch began life as Steve Baker Watch: a play on Net Zero Watch, the new name of the notorious climate denialist Global Warming Policy Foundation (mentioned earlier), of which Wycombe MP Baker was at the time a new trustee. Following a rejected attempt to persuade Baker to take up the climate cause, some of his constituents (Gemma Rogers, Stephen Morton, Tom Hardy and myself) founded the group, aiming to support local scrutiny of their MP's work to wreck government climate efforts; to challenge Baker's stance in the context of his slim 4,000 majority; and to seed a resilient, democratically minded network of local citizens. The energetic campaign that followed was tremendously popular, with demonstrations garnering local and national press coverage and celebrity support; additionally, a crowdfunder exceeded its target three times over, allowing campaign communications to reach every home in the constituency. Several other 'watch' groups have since launched in constituencies such as Thanet and Cumbria, with six more in incubation at time of writing. MP Watch aims to establish 100 groups in key constituencies before the next general election.

Crucially, MP Watch is unaffiliated to any political party and reaches out to people regardless of their political identity. We simply ask constituents an important question: 'Do you trust your MP with the future of your children?' Because this is effectively what they are doing. The scientists say that there is an existential threat that needs tackling now, and yet few politicians have stepped up to the mark. We encourage those who are unconvinced by their MP's actions to contact them and make their opinions felt – and if no action is forthcoming, they should strive to get another MP.

Many people love this idea, because it addresses the climate issue by tackling precisely the democratic deficit outlined above. By taking action, by engaging with other constituents who feel the same way, and by confronting their elected representative and holding them to account, voters are behaving less like consumers and more like active citizens: asking what their representation means and making it count. Experiencing success in influencing one's MP can awaken an appetite for 'citizening', which Jon Alexander compares to exercising a muscle.

We believe that the next general election represents a golden opportunity to shift the political culture of our country towards general acceptance of the urgency of achieving carbon net zero. Like all the 'small things' that will constitute 'the next big thing' in climate action, this attempt at bottom-up reinvigoration of political participation is not expected to be enough on its own. The transformation of political culture needed to bring system change is not linear, and it must be approached at multiple levels. But political change at the scale required by this crisis has no mandate without the active citizen. By building agency and connection among local people, and by uniting communities in a cause that goes beyond politics, we hope to help reenergize the citizenship paradigm that has lost its way, and which has never been more needed.

NOTES

1   See, for example, Kirk, E. (2022). The attention economy: standing out among the noise. *Forbes*, 23 March (www.forbes.com/sites/forbesbu sinessdevelopmentcouncil/2022/03/23/the-attention-economy-standi ng-out-among-the-noise/).

2   Alexander, J. (2022). *Citizens*. Cunbury.

3   See, for example, Devlin, K. (2022). Labour members back axing first-past-the-post despite Starmer opposition. *The Independent*, 26 September (www.independent.co.uk/news/uk/politics/labour-party-axe-first-past-the-post-b2175660.html).

4   Cadwalladr, C. (2019). Facebook's role in Brexit – and the threat to democracy. Ted Talk (www.ted.com/talks/carole_cadwalladr_face book_s_role_in_brexit_and_the_threat_to_democracy/transcript).

5   See, for example, Delahunty, S. (2020). The coronavirus crisis: corporations make moves to cynically exploit COVID-19. *Byline Times*, 12 May (https://bylinetimes.com/2020/05/12/the-coronavirus-crisis-corporations-make-moves-to-cynically-exploit-covid-19/).

6   See, for example, Centre for Public Impact (2019). Building consensus and compromise on Uber in Taiwan. Technology|Legitimacy article (www.centreforpublicimpact.org/case-study/building-consensus-com promise-uber-taiwan).

7   See, for example, Read, R. (2011). Are we a consumerist society – or a 'producerist' society? Article, 12 September (https://rupertread.net/ writings/2011/are-we-a-consumerist-society-or-a-producerist-society/).

CHAPTER 10

Let it sink in: combining science with emotional support creates climate action

A dialogue between Chamkaur Ghag and Liam Kavanagh

Chamkaur Ghag is a professor of astroparticle physics at University College London and a spokesperson for the world-leading Lux-Zeplin Dark Matter Experiment. Teaching environmental physics at UCL, he came to understand viscerally the climate threat facing humanity, its emotional impact on those who learn about it, and its potential to activate us given the right conditions. As a voice of the Climate Majority Project's climate anxiety campaign, he talks to Liam Kavanagh about scientific reticence and responsibility, the embodied journey of understanding climate, and what it takes to turn anxiety into participation in the greatest challenge the world has ever seen.

Chamkaur Ghag: I work on dark matter: trying to understand or detect the hypothesized stuff out there that makes up 85% of matter in the universe. I also began teaching the environmental physics course at UCL twelve years ago. In preparing the course material, I myself became properly educated on the climate crisis for the first time. It was an existential time. I had a new job, I was thinking about starting a family. But looking at the graph, I kept thinking: 'Wait … what? The curve only goes one way.' But then …surely not? Perhaps I was just being dramatic. If we were this close to extinction – what it means for food supplies, water, our supply chains, other mammals – I thought: 'Any minute now I'll learn that I'm making this huge error.' But of course it was all true.

As I learned, I felt fascination – but also fear. Anxiety. And a strange exhilaration: I wanted to teach this course well, to get through the physics of climate and environment, but I was impatient for the part where we introduce climate change and global warming. We've built a model of the environment: here's this rock, with this atmosphere, this depth, and the sun over here. What should the temperature be, once we've moved through all these phases? Once we're confident with our physical model, we pump some CO_2 in, and what happens? It's good for students to model for themselves and see how easily the equilibrium is disturbed.

It was life-changing. I stopped eating meat and did all sorts of other things. If I'm standing in front of these students saying 'these are the big contributors to climate change', I can't be a hypocrite. It was uncomfortable. Even though I was just passing on information, it was also touching me as a person. I started getting engaged in UCL's campaigns around setting net zero targets; what's happening on campus, etc.

Liam Kavanagh: So you're understanding climate from a first-person perspective, but *without any support*. You're an isolated person, studying this subject, fully capable of understanding it … with high confidence physically in what it means. But without anybody else around who understood.

CG: Yes – and feeling like I might be going insane because *why* is this not being reported with appropriate seriousness? For example, it takes just minutes to calculate what could happen to the Gulf Stream. This salinity, this fresh water, all this is moving over there … we see the decline, very, very clearly. Then if that happens, doesn't Europe get five to seven degrees cooler, just like that? *Surely not.* So you test again. Yes. Again. Yes. Every time. How am I not already reading about this? How have I reached this age without hearing that the Gulf Stream could damn near turn off? It's very similar to that *Don't Look Up* type scenario. And that's just *one* effect.

As I slowly opened up and spoke to colleagues about this, I started to sense that other people were also uncomfortable with the lack of open discussion. There's a big gradient: some people understand what's going on and the potential impact of what's coming, and they're wondering what should be done; some understand the science but *not* the impact; and some understand none of it. It felt good to at least get talking about it. But the anxiety and the existential crisis stuck around for a couple of years.

LK: We're touching on a tension that is central to this climate anxiety campaign that we're both working on: people don't want to disturb others by talking about the implications of science. You can't really be knowledgeable about the physical systems, investigate them thoroughly, without coming face to face with what's happening – right? So there's this potential tension between safeguarding the health of students or anybody who learns about this and the principles of education.

CG: In the early days students would pick up on the implications of what they were learning. And they would ask: 'Well, aren't we going to cover that?' As soon as students start asking *what this means*, it makes space to explore more deeply; it humanizes everything. For a time, when it came to, say, pollution, I'd say, put the textbook down, open the window and take a good lungful of the air on Euston Road. Now let's calculate what you just breathed in. The goal was really to take it out of the abstract – and that worked really well. Getting students 'embodied'; not just in their head thinking about what they need to remember for exams, but more present. Then it isn't the *student* listening; it's the *human* listening. There would be an exchange – from the formula and the equation to the climate science implications, and then to this palpable *sadness*. (There'd be avoidance as well. Some students who don't quite understand why others are breaking down or getting emotional.) I'd wonder, am I giving them *my* sadness? But no – because they're already aware, they kind of know. And here it is being reinforced. No, it's not just a bad dream. We're learning what it is, how we got here, and the scale of what we need to do.

LK: So students are coming in knowing on some level about what they're about to learn. And then during the class they basically find out that it's real.

CG: I think that's why some of them took the course to begin with. Most courses I've taught have been to physics students. But here we had arts and science students as well. And they were often so much more engaged. The impact of their felt emotion – the lymbic resonance or whatever – helped other students to open up. They'd get each other more curious. After a few years, throughout the course there would be a mass learning of the equations, etc., and then a mass sadness, and then sort of a mass *allowing* of the anxiety to be there, actually. Sometimes we hold off and we're just rational scientists. But at other times, you can't. We've actually got to stop, let this in and through us. Once the students did that – and perhaps what aided that process – was then asking: 'Okay, so what are we going to do about it?'

First there's education, then there's this crash, then there's this sort of rise-again, but with much higher enthusiasm than before for the job at hand. 'Here I am. I am a human. I had these ideas about what I might want to be or do, but actually I've been handed the job of all jobs' – right? If you want meaning in life, here you go! At some level it was even liberating. Some students are now in Antarctica. One's a UN ambassador. The usual 'I want to go into banking' or whatever became 'I want to go into a master's or a PhD in earth sciences or climate modelling … statistics … energy …'. There are so many areas where everyone could find something to do. Food, water, energy, social care, anxiety, medical – take your pick.

LK: There's this worry in climate education, climate communication that we don't want to depress people too much, and it comes at the expense sometimes of clarity and truth. So, for example, we're still talking about '1.5 is alive' as a climate goal. Almost no climate scientists believe that. Do *you* believe it?

CG: It's *long* gone. We fluctuated to 1.5 [1.5°C global average temperature rise above pre-industrial levels] this year. A few years ago, a paper reported a 50% probability of doing so in about the following five years. Eighteen months later, it had already happened. It had me questioning myself, thinking: 'Well, my projections say that things are a *lot* worse than this. But, hey, I'm a particle physicist, maybe I shouldn't be scrutinising. Maybe some statistical technique that they're using means it's actually not so bad.' But I could never quite figure it out.

Even the question of how quickly we would approach 1.5, I think, was really just a presentation issue for so long. We were projecting temperature out to 2100. I think this approach granted us some slack. We could play a bit with the numbers because the impact is all the way out there. It's for the grandkids. None of it ever stacked up to me.

And eventually the language came along about feedback loops and so on … and you think: 'Come, on, don't we *know* that?!' Doesn't everyone already know that if you have an ice cube it doesn't melt for a while, but once it starts melting, it's a puddle very quickly?

LK: Scientific reticence is a huge issue. Could deliberate emotional engagement, sharing and real emotional support help counteract that tendency to avoid putting two and two together? For climate scientists, for bureaucrats or people working in climate NGOs – anyone who has to engage with this stuff?

CG: Yes, I think it's necessary. Individuals need help and support to be able to educate others. The support needed for anybody trying to 'activate' is considerable. Some students are very … not even depressed, it's like someone's hit them over the head and they've fallen into nihilism. *This is all rubbish.* But then they can't settle even in that: even if you do push away the anxiety, it's still there unconsciously.

There's plenty you can say that's all doom and gloom. But there are also just ways of clearly presenting the science. And then there needs to be that pause to let it sink in, let it be there. And let the person feel it, because from there, the 'activation' into action, into will, is almost a power. There's a power generated from individuals wanting to do something. Not just because they're uncomfortable. But instead, taking it in, sitting with that and saying: 'Okay, it's not all on me. But what could I do?' And trying to align individual passion ... with an understanding that this is good for them. Not just to face it but really to let it pass through. If you do, you might find that beyond the fear there's potential, waiting to get cracking.

I think that empowers students. It's alright to be human. To want to fix everything. So many of us think at some point that it's *on* us individually. And that's what we've got to help people through. It's not the case. We're *all* in this. More and more will join. Don't worry about that – they won't have a choice. But for now we need some early pioneers who aren't as shook. When it really does start hitting the fan, we need people who can pass on that assurance: 'Yes it will get bad. Science is telling us so. But it's up to us to limit that as much as possible.'

And there's so much that can be done. It's going to get bad, and there *are* pathways where it's not *that* bad. We're unlikely to suddenly have things like decentralized solar panels and a global network next week, but I find it much more unlikely that it will *never* happen. Let's just get cracking and do it sooner. So many things. Desalination. Food growing. Having students think about this creatively is so much fun. Some of it is Star-Trek-level genius creativity. But then what do we do next year? How do we get there? Other students are very here and now. Eden-Project-like domes for growing, and so on.

LK: We say necessity is the mother of invention. Given how few people even in your department are totally clear about climate ... even you weren't until you taught the course and probably a lot of your colleagues aren't ... we have the people most capable of invention not actually knowing that there *is* a necessity, because essentially we're afraid of scaring people.

That brings us to a focus of the Climate Majority Project's anxiety campaign: knowing that the stakes are high is potentially hugely motivating, rather than terrifying, *if* you believe that you can do something *as part of a larger response*. [See, for example, 'Making the climate majority aware of itself' on pages 56–57.]

Churchill would say that hope must be built on solid and reasonable grounds. So as well as the truth, and people to handle it with, and an action we can take, we need this sense of being part of something larger. That last part is precisely what no psychologists provide in the experiments where they study responses to climate messages and find that people can get demotivated. When researchers say 'there's this really serious problem', they don't also say 'and there's a movement forming that recognizes our institutions are failing, and people from all walks of life are organizing, and challenging politics-business-as-usual – influential people from government, huge corporations, academia, etc.'. If you hear *that*, that's totally different, right? It's not you alone, the isolated experimental subject, one of billions of people who can't do anything.

CG: Yes. And the very first action that some of my students would take would be to pass on the knowledge, go home and talk to family – that energy immediately becoming kinetic energy. It was scientists behaving like scientists: sharing the knowledge. And learning that they're part of the greatest challenge there has ever been. I don't want to say 'excitement', but here's the opportunity to change all of the crap. From wars to subjugation in so many places and parts of society, over so many centuries. Here's how we end it. Climate change is affecting the whole planet: we *have* to cohere as one species and recognize that we have to care for the rest, that we depend on. Even for selfish reasons ... get compassionate! Human civilization has seen nothing like this – something that threatens the whole. If the whole is threatened, does the whole respond as one? And if the whole can respond as one, what *can't* we sort out – from hunger to poverty to resource distribution, right? It's a game changer.

I read recently some article from a union of concerned scientists about the economic benefit of leading on climate. *Argh!* While individual countries are still thinking about the economic benefit to them from climate leadership, it's still the old paradigm. *Share*, people! This won't be about who survived climate change with the most money. I don't think you understand the science here.

LK: In your experience, if people really let it sink in – what's at stake – do people think that way anymore?

CG: If it *really* sinks in? That thinking evaporates immediately. What does economic power over other countries mean if you're dependent on a redistributed supply chain? Materials, water, food, …

Look at energy. The sun shines enough on the earth in an hour to cover humanity's energy needs for a year. Of course we don't catch it all. But what if we catch a thousandth of it? Solar panels with a surface area the size of Nevada would do it. If they're all over the planet and they're hooked up – if we have energy-sharing through a decentralized distributed system – *we don't need batteries.* Because the sun is always shining somewhere. Losses in the cables? Have as much as you like. The sun gives a lot of energy. But then what does it mean for a city, say, in India to have cables crossing into Pakistan? What does it mean for a country to have power when you're sharing your … *power?* It's already the case with supply chains. *We're so interdependent,* but climate change brings it home in a way that's undeniable.

LK: The average person can notice the changing weather, but they can't imagine climate nonlinearities as easily as a physicist who deeply understands physical systems; who's trained to imagine them with great lucidity from the data. Denial is almost not an option for physical scientists. Isn't it then somehow their responsibility to play a role in communicating the consequences of climate change *emotionally*?

CG: I completely agree. When I first learned about climate change, it was all multiple colours and simulations running through my head. I've been doing this as a physicist for many, many years… After you see the first few data points, as a physicist or a physical scientist, the training or the innate part that likes analysing the data asks: 'What does this actually imply?'

But then sharing that with others? First there's the disembodied nature of our work; just living in the prefrontal cortex. That 'thought' part can park that data easily; it's very good at denying the implications or not wanting to look further. Scientists can gobble up the data, analyse it, do the projections, and then stop there, without letting it come back down and have meaning: 'Hey, you know your young child may never see a tiger?' That's just one weird example, but for me that's very stressful. It does something that I sense inside my body. It's not just a graph.

Surrounded by all of these illustrious scientists ... just speaking truth publicly about our situation and what could happen ... I imagine many scientists feel impostor syndrome. 'Who am I to do that?' We have to break out of this mindset. It's utterly untrue: not your job to go out there and speak science? Who told you that?

It hasn't been done so much in the past. We think we're these objective unbiased things, just over here analysing the data. But ... *is climate change not affecting you over there?* And at some level, perhaps they don't know that it is. But that's the job of education.

CHAPTER 11

Insuring our future? How insurers and the climate movement can find common cause

Rupert Read

The insurance industry faces existential risk as intensifying climate impacts threaten to create an uninsurable world. To ensure their own survival firms must adopt a precautionary approach, which means taking seriously their own and their clients' planetary impact and using their vast influence and financial power to curb environmental destruction. Avoiding ethical action will bring drastic financial consequences in the longer term, and legal and reputational damage will add to the price of delay. The sector has a critical role to play in gatekeeping bad actors, advocating policy changes and supporting climate initiatives. Insurers have a chance now to incentivize climate mitigation and adaptation, discriminating against harmful practices and investing properly in a sustainable future.

A strong business case for decisive climate action exists within many unlikely-sounding professions and industries, and activating that case is partly a task of storytelling. Powerful actors can be mobilized in the policy arena if they grasp and understand the depth of risk to their sector's viability, as well as their agency to effect change. Crucially, this approach need not be wholly mercenary, but can instead serve the ultimate double-bottom-line: ethical practice that makes good long-term business sense. Many industry executives are among the newly climate aware and are motivated to act from the perspective of their own ethical values. Joining the dots between climate and industry or key professions is a crucial communicative and organizing task of the Climate Majority Project.

The insurance industry offers an exemplary case. Insurance is a coping mechanism for vulnerability within our civilization.[1] We lessen the risk of individual disaster by pooling and sharing vulnerability, and reliance on this mechanism is baked into ordinary life. Insurance is therefore meaningful *to most people*: it is not a remote 'political' or 'activist' concern. It is a concern of the climate majority.

Many obvious points of alignment exist between an industry predicated on risk and a climate movement that seeks to avoid destabilizing the planet; in fact, it is no great stretch of the imagination to see the climate movement and the insurance industry as natural allies. Insurers are obliged to model the future, and their capacity to assess and underwrite risk is contingent on a certain degree of predictability. An increasingly volatile risk landscape threatens to destabilize business models that are founded upon a finite level of uncertainty and change. Increased frequency of acute outlier events – 'thousand year floods', for example – causes the risk of bankruptcy to rocket.

Uncertainty aside, a world of intensifying extreme weather and chronic climate impacts places unprecedented pressure on insurers in terms of claims, from business loss and property damage to crop failure. Conversely, escalating risk makes insurance unaffordable for clients and infeasible for insurers, depleting business for providers year on year. The wider societal impact of climate and environmental damage will also have a knock-on effect on health, life expectancy and other types of claim. Transitional risks will impact insurers' portfolios as assets are repriced.

In short: *insurance faces an existential risk*. As the world increasingly becomes uninsurable, insurance ceases to exist. In no other industry or profession is this as starkly and preemptively true. AXA is famously on record as saying that the world is on course to become uninsurable, much of it perhaps by as soon as the middle of this century. This process has already begun: State Farm Insurance recently announced that it will simply cease insuring property in California because of rising wildfire risks – a shocking announcement of a sort that could soon become commonplace.[2] An uninsurable world has, by definition, no place for an insurance industry.[3]

Industry executives are naturally aware of these issues, with many acknowledging that responding to climate risk is 'a top priority'. It is becoming common for consultants in the field to talk about 'adapting business models' to negotiate climate breakdown, but a wholly reactive approach suggests hopeless naivety about the scale of the problem. Instead, insurers need to operate according to the precautionary principle.

In 2019 the Net Zero Insurance Alliance was set up under the auspices of the UN to transition members' underwriting portfolios to net zero by 2050. The group's ambition and scope were relatively limited, not least because the 2050 target is of course hopelessly late. Membership peaked at thirty large insurers, but an exodus has recently been underway as companies react to criticism of environmental, social and governance (ESG) targets – and corporate social responsibility targets more generally – from extreme Republicans. This tragic failure borders on farcical: in truth, the Net Zero Insurance Alliance should have been criticized for being too timid rather than too bold.

Regardless of this recent demonstration of craven short-term thinking from industry 'leaders', the climate predicament will not simply go away for insurers. As economic damage from climate-linked events runs repeatedly into the hundreds of billions, insurers will be forced to consider the benefits of mitigation and adaptation as part of their own survival strategy. But a shift in vision and long-term logic is urgently needed for this truth to steer the industry from its current catastrophe-course. The insurance sector presents an important test case for climate majority strategy.

Beyond the industry case for financial self-preservation, such a strategy will also become necessary to support firms' reputations.

Insurers are in the business of calculating risk, and as a sector they are therefore uniquely well placed to foresee the severity of the complex climate impacts that are in store for society. They are, furthermore, in a position to share their knowledge, and to use their extraordinary financial power and influence to shift policy, benefiting their own sector while advocating changes that are a matter of survival for many. Failure to do so will attract scrutiny and vocal criticism from an increasingly powerful and broad-based climate movement, and experts who remain silent now will be judged harshly by publics suffering avoidable tragedies in years to come. Insurers claiming *not* to comprehend the level of approaching risk well enough to raise the alarm beyond their own boardrooms are guilty of catastrophic negligence, even on their own terms of due diligence.[4]

What is more, insurers are powerful enablers and de facto gatekeepers to many highly extractive and destructive industries, from fossil fuels to air freight and intensive agriculture. They are party to not only the risks these industries face but also to those they create. As such they are in a position to discriminate against harmful practices, penalizing those companies that pose the greatest risks to planetary health, and they can hope to emerge on the right side of history by doing so. Continuing to profit from those same processes will ultimately impact their public image, leading to a perceptible divergence between ethical and unethical insurers.

A neutral stance on climate and ecology will itself bring devastating financial consequences in the longer term. Failure to act ethically within this closing window of opportunity will result in legal action once consequences are felt by shareholders, by younger generations and by communities. Insurers will not be immune to the kind of actions brought against cigarette manufacturers and advertisers in previous generations – and today's increasing litigation against fossil fuel companies will find new targets tomorrow.

Conversely, insurers and their corporate social responsibility strategists might imagine proactively incentivizing climate mitigation and adaptation. Clear precedent exists for their intervention in policy where their own industry interacts systemically with another sector: for example, advocacy for individual health in the interests of medical insurance. They control huge sums of money, furthermore, that they are obliged to invest *in ways that protect their long-term financial value*. Insurers able to perceive their own interaction with matters of climate are thus empowered to become a force for good at this most precarious moment.

TOWARDS A CLIMATE MAJORITY TEMPLATE FOR INSURANCE

Insurance professionals can change the world by applying pressure on their companies to act in certain ways. Somewhat as Lawyers for Net Zero supports the general counsel of corporations to enforce their own companies to do the right thing, here we imagine a set of guiding principles that advocates within a serious 'Insurers for Net Zero' network might promote, to protect both their own best interests and those of the wider world.

- Tell the unvarnished truth about the climate dangers all customers are exposed to, now and over time. Disclose what they know about future rising risks and dangerous uncertainties.
- Act without delay, using the levers at their disposal to reduce the likelihood of those dangers, through choice of what they agree to insure and at what price. For example, insurance for climate-destructive enterprises like fossil fuel extraction and fossil fuel funding should become punitively expensive or simply unavailable, helping to 'strand' those assets. This is the kind of 'uninsurability' we really need to see.
- Place pressure on governments to reduce those dangers 'at source'. The lobbying power of insurers could be huge.
- Act responsibly and not acquisitively in relation to the vulnerabilities humanity is exposed to. For example, ordinary people should not be made to pay punitive insurance premiums for at-risk properties while coal mines can still find insurance.[5]
- Put the vast funds accrued from premiums (especially in life insurance) to work for the common good – i.e. strategic investment for a sustainable future and not just short-term, private profit – recognizing that such a future serves their own long-term interests. For example, consider actively supporting pragmatic,

effective climate initiatives. Strategic climate activators are the best prospect for an insurable future; and insurers control the wealth that can support them to function for mutual benefit.

The new 'moderate flank' strategy outlined in earlier chapters fundamentally depends upon individuals and networks of 'insiders' within the current system, driven by a radical shift in climate consciousness and pulling powerful levers for system change. This model is exemplified by the potential leverage of an insurance industry that is properly awake to the implications of the crisis and that is determined to bring change. The Climate Majority Project has begun working with figures inside the industry to accelerate the change that is in many ways inevitable, convening an informal group of those open to considering the kinds of idea discussed here, and in some cases already acting within their own organizations to insure our future. In the wake of the failed Net Zero Insurance Alliance, such a bottom-up strategy among those working in insurance is the most feasible way in which the industry can be encouraged to take an active role in climate leadership.

NOTES

1   Ludwig Feuerbach famously quipped that insurance companies obviated the need for religion!

2   Walker, A. (2023). California is becoming uninsurable. *Curbed*, 30 May (www.curbed.com/2023/05/state-farm-california-insurance-climate-change.html).

3   In the meantime, capital *allocation* for many risks should be (perhaps much) higher: insurers are exposed now to risks that even they do not fully comprehend in our uncertain new world. Setting aside more capital is crucial to protect against potential bankruptcy, a lesson they might learn from the position of banks in 2006 and the importance of higher capital allocation in crisis prevention.

4   Ugly insurance offers will emerge in the near future. Wall Street has already started offering 'hedges' to mitigate climate-related risks, essentially insuring some individuals against potential catastrophes that affect others. Much like credit default swaps before the financial

crisis, it is a dreadful concept. However, history has shown that such absurd ideas can temporarily sustain a failing system, ultimately placing us all at greater risk of catastrophe.

5   Only with a transition plan that, for example, supports people to relocate from areas at risk of rising sea levels and other factors, and penalizes the activities of businesses contributing to the growing uninsurability, could it be morally acceptable to declare ordinary people's properties uninsurable.

PART IV

DEEPER DIVES

CHAPTER 12

Wide awake in dreamland: shifting the public narrative on climate change

Marc Lopatin

As citizens we are stuck in a story, maintained by establishment voices, that there is always 'just enough time' to fix climate change. In reality, time is up. Deep and rapid institutional action is required if we are to limit damage and navigate instability, but as long as 'last warnings' postpone our understanding of how bad things really are, we will never form the mass mandate that unprecedented action requires. Shifting this stifling narrative begins with a plea from those citizens who are starting to realize that governments have failed. We are heading past 1.5°C of overheating, and it is time for leaders to level with the public, so they can get real on climate and demand change.

> In order to change things, we need everyone – we need billions of activists.
>
> — Greta Thunberg, May 2022

Here, Greta Thunberg once again displays her talent for cutting to the chase. To have a hope of steering civilization away from existential risk, citizen-led pressure for climate action needs to involve *most people*. But thus far, efforts to galvanize any such movement have scarcely scratched the surface.

This chapter is an invitation, nonetheless, to take this daunting call to action seriously. Not because it is necessarily possible to engage billions in the climate cause, but because if we dismiss that vision outright, there is little hope that governments and corporations will act meaningfully on climate science. Imagining this kind of mobilization is not an exercise in sheer make believe. Rather, it calls for honest enquiry into the forces that limit citizen agency and into how those forces might be overcome. What follows is a framework for such enquiry. A long list of committed environmentalists, politicians and experts have of course been trying to mobilize the public for many years. It is instructive, however, that the most attention-grabbing intervention to date – Extinction Rebellion's gatecrashing of the mainstream in April 2019 – was premised on *avoiding* the need for active support from a majority of people.

XR's theory of change called for the involvement of just 3.5% of the population as a precursor for achieving its transformative aims. The target was appealing, perhaps, because it liberated XR from having to worry about the rest of us.

That is not to say that the rest of us are hardened climate deniers. On the contrary, polling repeatedly shows people *are* concerned about climate change and the natural world.[1] But that concern is often accompanied by a generalized sense of powerlessness. The psychological discomfort that comes from feeling both responsible for and ultimately unable to do anything about the crisis brings people close to overwhelm, making them feel deeply unsafe. This means that the majority of people routinely evade or discount the tales of catastrophe that are thrust their way by climate activists.

The tendency to prioritize stories about the world that keep us safe from sudden or transformative change is central to this chapter. In short, we are all ears for the story that we want. In the case of dangerous anthropogenic global warming, the public story has shifted over decades from it being not real, not serious, not human-induced to being very serious but fixable.

Each pivot in the climate narrative is 'sponsored' by a set of institutions that act as storytellers-in-chief. It has the feel of an improvised dance, inspired by both audience and storyteller wanting to feel safe from a common threat. I call this dance mutually assured protection (MAP).

MAP can operate on multiple levels: it can be below the radar and indulge in malicious falsehood, or it can be out in the open and culturally sanctioned. As we will discuss, both approaches have conspired to save audience and storyteller alike from getting real about climate action for decades.

MAP 1.0: BIG OIL'S PYRRHIC VICTORY

In 2023 it is certainly no secret that Big Oil has successfully frustrated the efforts of scientists to secure government action on climate. But how was their network of think tanks, lobbyists and public relations companies so staggeringly successful for so long?

Big Oil had an incentive to tamper with the story as soon as climate science began to emerge seventy years ago: a future without oil was, and remains, an existential fear for the industry. That led to a highly incentivized sector of the global economy asking itself a simple but profound question: what do *we* need to tell the outside world about climate change to make us *all* feel better? MAP 1.0 was born.

Big Oil correctly identified that the general public would be willing to believe global heating did not exist, or at least did not require them to act. It might break the hearts of scientists and environmentalists, but this was always – and continues to be – the story that people want to hear.

Of course, Big Oil is not solely responsible for decades of climate inactivism, but it concerned itself more than anyone else with maintaining the gap between climate science on the one hand and humanity's collective response on the other. Oil companies did this by deliberately setting out to tell stories that spared themselves and the general public from having to confront and act on reality.

Over the decades, Big Oil was forced to concede ground as observed science confirmed the earliest research and climate modelling. But rather than these breakthrough moments culminating in an overdue reality check of the seriousness of the threat to civilization, something else happened instead: MAP *evolved*.

As outright climate denialism fell out of mainstream favour, governments, business, academia and countless other institutions were suddenly saddled with their own existential threat from climate change. And it cut far deeper than maintaining markets for liquid fossil fuels. This time, what was at stake was the very survival of business-as-usual: perpetual economic growth, buoyed by unfettered consumption and extraction of all that the planet has to offer.

Seriously addressing the threat of catastrophic climate change was heretical for the simple reason that it would require unprecedented systems-level change of a kind that would render business-as-usual unrecognizable – even largely obsolete. Hence the oft-cited quote: 'It is easier to imagine the end of the world than the end of capitalism.'

So while the Big Oil executives of the 1960s shuddered at a vision of a world without fossil fuels, twenty-first-century leaders – spanning politics and just about every sector of the world economy – shuddered at the prospect of business-as-usual being one day banished in the struggle to retain a liveable planet.

And so, in their own distributed and semi-unconscious way, institutions across the board began asking themselves: what does the world need to hear that will make *everyone* feel better? The answer: 'Yes, climate change is urgent. No, we have not done enough. Yes, there is enough time to fix it.'

MAP 2.0: #YESWECAN

It would be churlish to claim that the evolution of MAP did not represent progress of a sort. Admitting that human-induced climate change urgently needs tackling is better than denying it even exists as a problem. But, because MAP 2.0 transmits the message that business-as-usual has got the matter in hand, the impact on the public of this institutional 'call to arms' has been stultifying. In other words, the people are being given the story that they want.

Witness world governments in 2015 agreeing to restrict average global temperature rise to 'well below 2°C'. In the real world, carbon emissions that continue to grow year on year make a mockery of such pledges. But then, as the saying goes, never let the facts get in the way of a good story.

Enter the Intergovernmental Panel on Climate Change (IPCC) to rescue the political situation in 2018 by issuing fantastical emissions reduction pathways to keep politically agreed climate goals alive.[2] The IPCC stated that to have even a 50% chance of preventing average global temperature rise from exceeding 1.5°C by the century's end, global fossil fuel emissions would have to be almost halved between 2018 and 2030. Five years on (in March 2023) the IPCC issued world governments with a 'final warning' to complete the same task in less than seven years. (Incidentally, global energy demand is assumed to rise over the same period.) Such is the outright implausibility of the 'final warning', one wondered whether the IPCC had issued a silent scream for 'de-growth'. Unlikely. Not least because the IPCC's emissions reduction pathways rely on 'overshoot', which permits average temperature to go above 1.5°C for a period of decades before falling back down beneath the threshold by the century's end. Such pathways are premised on the future deployment of carbon dioxide removal (CDR) technologies to remove previously emitted CO_2 from the atmosphere.

But here is the rub: the sanctioning of future overshoot opens up present-day, 'scientist-sponsored' permission space for leaders across politics, business and the environmental movement to continue talking up net zero by 2050, or visions of 'green growth' or a 'just transition'.

The less-talked-about aspect of these pleasing visions is that they bet the house on fully scalable and optimized CDR technology arriving on time and on budget (circa 2050) to scrub the air free of the billions of tonnes of CO_2 that, under business-as-usual at least, will be emitted for decades to come.

None of this puts a dent in MAP 2.0 however. In place of realism, an insistence on optimism polices the mainstream climate change narrative. You have been exposed to it over and over. When we are told it is 'our last best chance' or that it is 'now or never'; when people say 'we have the technologies' or that the heating is 'reversible if we act now', and so on. And it is upheld by just about everyone the public looks to inform them and tackle climate change: politicians, CEOs, scientists, journalists and green NGOs. Proponents of a 'stubborn optimist' view tend to argue that political and economic momentum is finally building around global climate action, and any sudden admission of the mess we are *really* in could derail the whole project.³

But the upshot seems to be that, whereas MAP 1.0 put clear blue water between, say, fossil-fuel-funded climate denial on the one hand and scientists on the other, the public is today presented with establishment-wide agreement that no matter how messed up the weather gets, there is always time left to fix it. There is intense disagreement, of course, about how to go about the fixing part. It goes without saying that Greenpeace and Royal Dutch Shell, say, have competing visions of the future, but this is reduced to second-order stuff. Tomorrow never comes when cultural time is frozen at five to midnight.

Uninterrogated optimism harbours a fatal contradiction. To elicit the required political will for deep and difficult change, the climate movement absolutely needs vigorous and enthusiastic backing from most citizens. Yet sponsors of stubborn optimism undo their noble aims by reassuring the public – at the all-important institutional level – that despite climate change being 'out of control',⁴ everything can *still* be ok.

The same contradiction bedevils advocates of technological solutions, who look to optimized markets over muscular state intervention. Why are climate-concerned investors not yet funnelling trillions of dollars their way to reengineer 'tomorrow's world'? One reason is that hundreds of millions of citizens are yet to collectively express demand for their vision of technological salvation. The public is simply not feeling – or not acting out – the urgency: an outcome that is baked into MAP 2.0.

I am not suggesting that all of society allows authorities to simply spoonfeed them a narrative that keeps them blithely unaware. Rather, it is the more subtle scenario where, as long as society is deceiving itself at an institutional level, there is permission to do the same at a personal level: people choose whichever story allows them to protect themselves from the nagging reality of the situation and the need to initiate change. The content of this story can vary widely, as the Climate Majority Project's own audience research has demonstrated. Asked about their relationship with the crisis, some people report that they are already doing their bit (by recycling; by cutting back on meat) while others express knee-jerk doomism (it is too late; we are screwed).

The point is that *whatever* people tell themselves under MAP 2.0 doubles as permission to carry on doing the same, whether it is 'I'm doing my bit', 'I don't know what to do?' or, indeed, 'What's the point, we're doomed'. The result is that business-as-usual triumphs at both the personal and institutional levels. To borrow a line from 1980s US singer–songwriter Pat Benatar: we are wide awake in dreamland.

In dreamland, nothing in the institutional telling of the climate change story can end in failure or loss. So the now-impossible 1.5°C limit will still be nursed from one COP summit to the next like some absent, aged ruler that everybody in the palace knows is dead but whose continued existence is required to prop up the regime.

MAP 2.0 picks up where its predecessor left off, by continually signalling permission to the general public that everyone can carry on doing the same thing. Not only does this run counter to what many climate scientists and other insiders privately admit, it also, more importantly, eats up society's response time for meaningful climate action. Investors know this phenomenon by another name: opportunity cost.

This delay is already contributing to what researchers have labelled a climate 'doom loop',[5] the conditions for which are created by present-day government failure to reduce global carbon emissions at anything like the rate that the IPCC sets out. Absence of mitigation leads to snowballing costs from, for example, extreme weather and human migration. Dealing with the fallout from these things forces governments to throttle back, or even abandon, efforts to cut greenhouse gas emissions, leading to yet more climate impacts and even bigger economic burdens in the future.

MUTUALLY ASSURED PROTECTION 3.0?

If a leap in public agency is needed to help avert a doom loop, it will require the displacement of MAP 2.0. Bringing this displacement about is the purpose of People Get Real (PGR), an incubated start-up of the Climate Majority Project.[6]

PGR operates under the premise that action on climate change is beset by vicious circles – among them the tendency of both the public and institutions to limit each other's agency thanks to stories that sustain business-as-usual. But wherever such a circular relationship exists, there lives the potential to reverse the process and create a virtuous circle, where each party provides permission to the other to grow and overcome what was previously culturally sanctioned.

Hopefully, we are agreed that mass citizen support is a necessary condition for the deep and rapid institution-led action we need. But what on earth can shift the climate narrative while response time still matters? We have seen all too clearly that despite intuition to the contrary, possession of new facts does not automatically precipitate action. Rather, we need mass agency *and* a new story, each advancing and strengthening the other.

PGR sees a creative opportunity to inspire an incremental but ultimately mass defection from the official five-to-midnight narrative. Imagine, for example, a campaign that empowers citizens to make the first move in shifting the mainstream climate narrative towards truthfulness. Granting that many people know intuitively that the trouble goes far deeper than is publicly acknowledged, early participants, running into thousands, might be supported to issue a joint challenge to trusted institutional figures to tell the truth.

Of course, 'trusted institutional figures' are not the usual suspects: governments and oil companies. I refer here to more unusual suspects, including the climate expert community, pro-climate leaders from business and politics, and even the environmental movement itself. All could be publicly invited to 'level with us' about the real situation with climate change.

Why shine a light on those whom the public already trusts on climate? Well, the potential 'defection' from the five-to-midnight story by well-known environmental figures, trusted scientific institutions and even major brands would be both countercultural and newsworthy. In response, mainstream media – encouraged by this and by campaign pressure – might begin making more space for (hitherto outlier) experts challenging green-tinted business-as-usual thinking. As the stifling five-to-midnight narrative is displaced further, yet more citizens would be freed to become active, growing the campaign, and so on, in a virtuous feedback loop.

The loop is established by aggregating citizen participation – through individual 'micro-asks' – to exert collectivized pressure on target institutions and influential figures, whose positive responses can generate further citizen participation in turn. The 'micro-ask' might even take a familiar form, such as joining an email campaign or signing a petition, say. It is the target of each campaign, however, that differentiates it from traditional NGO approaches. Indeed, influential NGOs might themselves be the subject of campaigns, as per the genius occupation of Greenpeace's London headquarters by XR in October 2018.[7]

Instead of bashing tone deaf governments or nefarious oil companies, PGR will focus its attention on other sectors and institutions that are displaying a culture of self-deception. This work could include anonymously polling climate experts, environmentalists, the sustainability profession, the insurance sector or even the heads of marketing across the FTSE 100. The intention each time is to show the public what trusted figures privately believe about climate action. Such tactics are part of breaking down the establishment-wide insistence that there is still time to fix the climate. It is ultimately to isolate governments and fossil fuel interests for all citizens to see.

To do this, PGR and its partners will seek to develop and test campaigns capable of empowering citizens in the first instance to issue the challenge, encouraging them to see that their own participation is ultimately what brings *more* people onboard.

Such a campaign would need to validate feelings of overwhelm and powerlessness while gently challenging such self-protection with a 'no-brainer' call to action. It should offer a compelling vision of participation in a growing effort to (i) dismantle the feedback loop that keeps people in their chairs and (ii) build what CMP co-director Rupert Read has termed a 'mass wave or happening' that can wield genuine power.

Just as a sense of powerlessness contributes to avoidance, among the best ways to help people cope with difficult news is by empowering them to do something about it – preferably together. Thus, with PGR we aim to bring about MAP 3.0: 'Yes, climate change is no ordinary emergency. Yes, we all know it is too late to keep warming within "safe" limits. Yes, it is time to stop telling ourselves there is nothing we can do, and to get busy.'

NOTES

1   DESNZ Public Attitudes Tracker: net zero and climate change (Spring 2023;   https://assets.publishing.service.gov.uk/government/uploads/system/uploads/attachment_data/file/1164127/desnz-pat-spring-2023-net-zero-and-climate-change.pdf).

2   IPCC (2018). Global warming of 1.5°C. Special Report (www.ipcc.ch/sr15/).

3   Solnit, R. (2023). We can't afford to be climate doomers. *The Guardian*, 26 July (www.theguardian.com/commentisfree/2023/jul/26/we-cant-afford-to-be-climate-doomers).

4   Euronews (2023). 'Climate change is out of control' warns UN chief as Earth suffers hottest week on record. *Euronews*, 7 July (www.euronews.com/green/2023/07/07/climate-change-is-out-of-control-warns-un-chief-as-earth-suffers-hottest-week-on-record).

5   Laybourn, L. *et al.* (2023). 1.5°C – dead or alive? The risks to transformational change from reaching and breaching the Paris Agreement goal. Report, IPPR (www.ippr.org/research/publications/1-5c-dead-or-alive).

6   See https://peoplegetreal.org/.

7   Molitch-Hou, M. (2018). Climate activists occupy Greenpeace UK headquarters – wait, that can't be right. *Common Dreams*, 19 October (www.commondreams.org/views/2018/10/19/climate-activists-occupy-greenpeace-uk-headquarters-wait-cant-be-right).

CHAPTER 13

Inner work for a climate-aware majority

Liam Kavanagh

Feeling the gravity of climate breakdown tends to bring on soul searching, as does the experience of reaching across the political chasms of our polarized society. Conversely, it is often that capacity for inner reflection that reveals and strengthens our interconnection with ourselves, with others and with our crisis-hit world, unlocking the love, insight and collective resilience that gives us the strength to act.[1] And little of this hard work is possible at all without finding joy, in spite of our predicament. Inner work is therefore inseparable from the climate response. This chapter makes the case that inner work is a practical necessity for mainstream climate action, it suggests practical ways to support inner work in the climate majority, and it points readers towards learnings and recurring issues from inner work in the climate movement. It also considers how to avoid making inner work inaccessible, or even a barrier, to those outside the traditional 'climate bubble'.

Perhaps you are asking what 'inner work' is. The word 'inner' points towards parts of life that cannot be seen, touched, grabbed, eaten or bought. Experiences like loss and turbulent love often precipitate intense inner work, but nobody is without inner work in their life. Stopping to feel the moment more deeply is inner work. Examining our hopes, fears and self-images to see if they are well founded is inner work. Singing can be a form of inner work, as can prayer, meditation and long intimate talks with friends in a time of need. So too can be twelve-step programmes and support groups, and an athlete's practice of 'keeping calm under pressure' on big stages. In fact, inner work stretches across every field of endeavour, as we are informed by innumerable statements that 'this game/business/skill/ art is mainly mental/emotional/spiritual'.

Though the distinction between 'inner' and 'outer' feels very real to us, 'inner' feelings are part of a human response to any outer event. It is easier to *ignore* feelings, or even thoughts attached to events, than it is to ignore 'concrete' observations, but they are no less important. How we feel determines how we act.

Still, many find the mere mention of 'inner work' awkward. In our secular society, discussion of inner affairs is typically reserved for private settings, while public discussion tends to focus on tangible matters. Inner work was at one time synonymous with religion, and it still carries that association;[2] at other times it can be considered a mental health 'issue'. Inner work is sometimes seen as a wasteful distraction from more tangible pursuits. These associations mean that inner work must be spoken about carefully, in a way that fits different audiences and situations. In climate action, as in other spheres, most of us who do inner work as part of our vocation do not talk about inner work, much less advocate for it, but it has a long history in the environmental movement.

Before moving on, I would like to reassure nervous readers that I will not try to convince you to use the specific term 'inner work'. The term is imperfect, though I doubt another clever name will pick out the same kind of activities that 'inner work' does while avoiding awkward feelings. This becomes clear when we explore why inner work is an almost unavoidable part of truth and climate action.

INNER WORK FOLLOWS FROM TRUTHFULNESS

There is good news and bad news about inner work and truth. The good news is that inner work can help us get in touch with the meaning and joy that come from doing work that is necessary for future generations. The bad news, of course, is that in climate action, as in many walks of life, people are most often brought into inner work through loss. Dealing with very bad news is part of climate action, and thus, so is inner work. Common words associated with 'climate' include crisis, denial and anxiety – all indisputably states of inner life. So the work of navigating these states is the partner of knowledge about our predicament, and knowledge of the meaning of climate action. Anybody who doubts this should speak to students. Educators are increasingly seeking to integrate counselling with climate education because the facts are so inherently distressing – and motivating. So if building a climajority requires truth, it requires inner work.

Climate communicators' official 'wisdom' tells us not to dwell on disturbing realities[3] – the kind that might plunge the audience into inner work, as happens involuntarily after somebody dies or our dreams are broken and our life is 'turned upside down'. Climate communicators are supposed to help their audience avoid the dreaded sense of powerlessness, where we feel unable to stop chaos that has been slowly approaching for about thirty-five years. Messages should allegedly never lead us, the audience, to despair about the messy state of our political system – which is, after all, our means of making collective plans. Communicators therefore turn the audience's attention to a concrete action that *feels* like a response to the climate emergency. Recycling more, for example, or flying less. The audience are not asked to 'stay with the trouble',[4] therefore, but to instead move quickly away to (insufficient) action – and stay there. Moving directly to action can 'bypass' distress efficaciously, it is claimed.

HELPING TRUTHFULNESS BECOME APPROPRIATE ACTION

From a certain angle, helping people avoid the trouble may seem like the compassionate approach, but is it sustainable? If there were a grand and genuinely well-formed plan to follow, perhaps we could all just immerse ourselves in action straight away. But the official plan still relies, to a discouraging extent, on more COP meetings, on waiting for technology to save us, and on campaigns to nudge individual consumer choice. Acceptable and respectable actions will not work to actually create transformative change, rapidly and at scale. We will have to look at the trouble fully in order to create a plan that is sufficient to address it. If we merely glance at it, it will grow and force us to look again.

To put it bluntly, the rush to action – a point of pride for many – can often be driven by an impulse to avoid the difficulty of staring the crisis in the face. Action is obviously called for, but we will act more effectively and appropriately if we are able to face fear, discomfort and the magnitude of the task than we will if we distract ourselves from our fears by focusing so tightly on our personal actions that we fail to see anything else.

HOW ACTION CAN BECOME AVOIDANCE

When we feel isolated or too small to make a difference and cannot make peace with the mess we are in, dysfunctional reactions can occur: overwork and tunnel vision (trying to do more than is humanly possible), for example, or exaggerating the importance of our strategy (magic bullet-ism) or inflating our personal abilities (saviour complex.) All of these make us feel more in control of the situation. These are occupational hazards of climate action, which can occur in a person who is actually doing quite a lot of good, tangible work. The world's future is at stake, after all, and strong emotions do therefore arise and feed these kinds of distortions.

Similarly, the temptation to exaggerate the importance or completeness of the particular organization we are involved in is an emotional challenge, and one that is too little discussed. Because we want to do something significant about the threat posed by climate change, we want to be part of an effort that can address this vast issue. A good idea that is worth trying can too easily become *the plan*: a road to salvation.

For this reason, pathbreaking groups such as XR and Transition Towns, as well as inspiring climate leaders, can *also* (unwittingly) help their 'followers' avoid staying with the trouble. As soon as people have a plan that tells us how to act, we can think about the trouble less, at least for a while. Leaders usually provide plans and organize others to implement them. The leaders' job is also to believe deeply in a plan, so that others can too. The desire among members for confidence in an organization can even subtly encourage its leaders to develop inflated egos and can drive overconfidence about their plan.

The leaders of large organizations and movements who think about the imposingly big and complex picture often cannot avoid doubts and ambiguities, while 'followers' can avoid feeling the trouble too intensely by immersing themselves deeply in their tasks. Whether we like it or not, the trouble comes back and finds us, because the brilliant theories of change and the challenging actions offered – whether they are mass street protests, worldwide transition town-by-town, or Paris Treaty commitments – are at best pieces of a vast puzzle. Furthermore, if we need to feel that we have 'the answer', then other people's (very useful) plans can even become threats to our own.

We need humility and confidence in a wider movement. A decentralized movement with many leaders working on many distributed, coordinated initiatives will require many people who are able to sit with the trouble and who are able to change their aspect of the plan if it is not working. In order to plan together, we need to stay with trouble together.

Finally, it is important to note that overwork is a great distraction from our emotions but that it usually ends in burnout. Whether work becomes therapeutic 'action therapy' or exhausting martyrdom comes down to the inner work of humility, being kind to ourselves and accepting the limits of what we can do. We must all accept that we are part of something larger and that we need others. We can do the best that we can and no more.

A COMMUNITY FOR INNER WORK IS ALREADY HERE, AND IT IS GROWING

As already mentioned, many people have been on the emotional journey to climate awareness over quite a long period. Communities whose members support each other through rising awareness of climate and wider societal crises have therefore formed all around the world, among diverse demographics. The most simple and effective

way to promote the collective inner work needed is to raise the profile of the space for inner work that has already developed, helping
more people join it and get help.

Whether you are a climate-concerned atheist, an agnostic, a person of religion or irreverent, there are places for inner work that will
welcome you, at least online if not in person. The Climate Psychology Alliance offers spaces such as Climate Cafes, where people simply share their concerns about climate openly in a welcoming environment. Artists have, for generations, created work inspired by the
ecological crisis. The co-founder of the Green Party, the legendary
artist Josef Beuys, is one, but there are many others, too numerous to
count. Buddhists have long been working on practices for ecological
awareness, especially since Joanna Macy's *The Work That Reconnects*
in the 1980s (which has now spread across the world). Macy's work
has aided participants in grappling with their anger, sadness, numb-
ness and fear to find joy and purpose in work. It has also inspired
many who depart from Macy's Buddhist-infused language and
imagery, mainstreaming and expanding on her efforts. Phoebe Tickell's *Moral Imaginations* is a particularly interesting recent example
in the UK. Environmental movements have also recognized the
importance of inner work, such as the Inner Transition programme
started by Transition Towns in 2006, and their subsequent Carbon
Conversations initiative.

After we start to accept our situation and find a community that
does the same, a whole new world of meaningfulness and camarade-
rie starts to open up.

FINDING A CLIMATE CALLING:
THE IMPORTANCE OF INTUITION

For many, awakening climate awareness is followed by a challenging
and exciting process of finding the work that is ours to do. This
process takes – to paraphrase the 'Serenity Prayer' – the serenity to
accept what we can't change and the courage to change what we can.
Accepting our limits, and still finding devoted work that is ours,
requires a humble reflection on ourselves and the situation, and very
often a 'leap of faith' into unknown waters.

Science does not yet explain well where intuition comes from, though contemporary science of the mind accepts that there is such a thing, and that it is valid and valuable. Intuition is a quality that helps us navigate spaces too complex to be broken down with clear and simple logic. Learning to attune ourselves to this inner compass is a vital part of our inner work.[5] The rising climate majority is being advanced by many who have ignored the need for respectable metrics of success and followed an intuition that something new was required. Such intuitive feelings precede breakthroughs in every field, whether that is art, business, science or politics. Finding our work is not easy, and in dynamic contexts this process never stops. Environmental action is just such a field.

Climate action organizers cannot tell everybody what to do, but all of us could use help to find our path with as little suffering as possible. Help is out there: immersive retreats such as 'The Edge', offered by Kimberley Hare of HEART Community Group, support people on this journey, as do similar offerings from people such as Rupert Read, Jem Bendell and Katie Carr of Deep Adaptation, Margaret Wheatley and 'Warriors for the Human Spirit', Shaun Chamberlin and many others. Bringing together these practitioners to discuss best practices is also an important aim.

CONNECTING BY WIDENING PERSPECTIVES

As people inquire into the roots of climate breakdown, many come to see it as part of a wider problem that has important 'inner' elements. The word 'polycrisis' is becoming mainstream. Once the preserve of avante-garde systems theorists, the term recently made the front page of the *Financial Times*.[6] This idea suggests that political turmoil, 'culture wars', military conflicts and economic tensions are intertwined with the environmental crisis at a deep level. Many see a moral or 'spiritual' crisis at the heart of all this,[7] and that moral crisis is increasingly perceived as rooted in a lack of felt connection or relationship among people, and between people and life on earth.

This demanding subject needs a book-length treatment, but it is worth noting a few points here. Firstly, cultivating felt connection is core to inner work that is revered within the environmental movement. Secondly, programmes of inner working to create felt (inter) connection can both create intense motivation and also divide people. At present this work is often perceived as being 'for progressives', 'for leftists', 'for elites', etc. Furthermore, the emotions that come from connection to endangered lives are challenging, especially in politically diverse groups.

Many environmentalists have long felt that *disconnection* from a felt importance of other lives, including non-human life and nature, is part of a consumerist, growth-driven society, making environmental crises inevitable. Increased connection and appreciation of the innate value of life means an increased incentive to address climate change and the biodiversity crisis[8] as well as wars, political divides and poverty. Macy's *The Work That Reconnects* has become a favourite practice for cultivating a sense of connection to future generations and other species, featuring imaginative exercises, expressions and roleplay. This and similar beliefs and practices are meaningful and motivating to many environmentalists but may sound 'abstract' or 'mystical' to others.

The notion that a sense of connection to other lives will help with the climate crisis is not hard to argue for more widely, however. Naturalists such as David Attenborough, as well as countless artists, take a version of this view. Scientific evidence on how this connection can be built, and how it affects environmental attitudes, is laid out in 'Reconnection: Meeting the Climate Crisis Inside Out', a 2022 report from the Mindfulness Initiative,[9] and efforts inspired by Macy's work but more geared towards the mainstream, such as Tickell's *Moral Imaginations*, are expanding every year.

At the same time, there are hurdles to widespread 'reconnection'. Science's power to persuade is not universal: for example, it has taken thousands of mindfulness studies over two decades to help a large subset of Britons (approximately 15%) to develop an active mindfulness practice and to bring openness to the idea into the mainstream. We should not bank on 'reconnection' to all living beings becoming mainstream on the timescale that is needed to respond to the climate crisis. And, at this late stage, many of us, especially the young, need only to be connected to our own future to acquire motivation to respond to the climate crisis. Questions about what level of connec-tion is necessary are therefore likely to become contentious, though developing a wider circle of concern is also important for addressing biodiversity and other concerns.

Herein lies the difficulty: how will a mainstream climate move-ment incorporate people with diverse levels of felt connection to lives far removed from their own? Feelings of connection to other lives have political and economic consequences. Arguably, Attenbor-ough's subtle message of interconnection can only become so popu-lar because, in contrast with the global justice movement, it does not dwell on appreciating the lives of other people, especially citizens of the Global South. 'Connecting' to the consequences of empire can quickly become a source of division among climate-aware people.

None of this means we should discourage connection, or encour-age *only so much of it.* Unfortunately, I do not see a clear answer to this thorny problem, but a few observations are worth making. Firstly, appreciation of all life is a great task – one that the world's wisdom traditions have undertaken for millenia – and progress here will help climate action. However, mass enlightenment is not necessary to address dangerous climate change, and we should not plan around it, strategically. Secondly, the highest ideals of wisdom traditions include connection to those who do not appreciate other lives very much at all. The difference between valuing a lifeform and approving of its behaviour may seem subtle, but it is vast.

To see oneself as deeply connected with others while still passionately asking them to change their behaviour is possibly the most difficult inner challenge we face, and we should never underestimate the difficulty of it. Martin Luther King, Gandhi and Nelson Mandela provide us with famous examples,[10] but their lasting impression shows that these abilities are as rare as they are inspiring. By, for example, dismissing others because they do not exhibit the highest appreciation of all life, we are not following the example of these great teachers. We also need to avoid dismissing anybody simply because they (for instance) 'virtue signal'. The nature of our longest traditions of inner work is to aspire towards ideals that few people obtain; nobody needs to be perfect, or free of hypocrisy, to be appreciated.

SHARED UNDERSTANDING IS ALSO INNER WORK

The process of coming to a shared understanding is often thought of as an almost exclusively intellectual activity, but this is just another way in which the inner and emotional dimension of things can be minimized. When dealing with complex issues it is important to maintain humility, and to remember that we might be wrong. Creating shared understanding also means having the ability to see that not all views make an equal amount of sense and to stand firm for views that make a great deal of sense.

The ability to let go of views that have come to be very important to us, and to consider others, is again an inner challenge that wisdom traditions have addressed for millenia. Getting in touch with our need to be right or morally superior and relaxing it is a skill that most of us instinctively practise at times. We will need a great deal of this skill in order for very different worldviews to work side by side to address dangerous climate change.

And there is more.

The variety of inner work that is useful for the climate and environmental emergency is vast, and this short chapter makes only a very simple case for this intangible sort of work. There is no time to discuss the fact that humans' ability to overcome fear is probably much greater than most imagine, for example. Moreover, it seems certain that we are capable of being far more joyful than we are now without requiring economic growth, which would ensure that a better future is possible, regardless of whether we decouple growth from pollution. All of these topics have, however, been explored in depth by others.

A FLOTILLA FOR INNER WORK

In chapter 3, Rupert Read and I suggest that mainstream climate action is more likely to be driven by a gathering of organizations, etc., that share a common cause rather than by one big organization or entity. Shared inner work will necessarily be similar, with many quite different communities and organizations working together – or independently – on the things they can agree on. Attitudes towards inner work are personally and culturally sensitive, with sharp differences in the language and practices that people gravitate towards. It would be extremely challenging to come up with a single kind of community support or personal practice that any member of the mainstream climate movement can do.

PROMOTING INNER WORK

One way of promoting this work to the millions who are experiencing dangerous anthropogenic climate change is, of course, to simply draw the attention of people who are concerned about the climate/polycrisis to existing work through media campaigns, articles and websites. In our opinion, however, a more ambitious route is possible.

The current state of inner work is a lot like that of 'sustainability' in the 1990s. Many were doing work that would shortly be known as sustainability, but under different names. Without a chorus repeating the same name, a public identity had not taken hold. Soon after this identity was formed, sustainability became 'a thing'. The time is ripe for a similar shift in the area of inner work, and some efforts are underway. A concerted campaign to forge a name and identity is necessary, as well as a media campaign to broadcast that identity across grassroots networks of people doing climate resilience work, news media and academia, to make (psychological as well as material) inner work 'a thing' in the public imagination.

THE VALUES OF AN EFFECTIVE CLIMATE MAJORITY

For deep societal change to happen, we eventually need a majority of the population on the same side, which means bridging the divides of our polarized societies. This work is as much an inner challenge as climate awareness is, and it stretches our minds and hearts in challenging – but ultimately rewarding – ways. To avoid becoming trapped in polarizing dynamics, with all parties locked in cycles of mutual reflexive defensiveness and hostility, an effective advocate for climate action will be in touch with their own triggers and ego trips. Navigating such tensions requires us to respect people despite differences, to build coalitions rather than winning wars of ideas, to relinquish feelings of 'ownership' around the climate issue, to meet people where they are, and to have patience. All of these are challenging practices, and the first step is to forgive ourselves for failing to live up to our own aspirations, as we inevitably will.

RESPECT AND TOLERANCE

Differences in political ideology, cultural background or knowledge are all challenging, but if we let them breed contempt we cannot build the movement that we need. Respect does not mean avoiding disagreement, but avoiding animosity. In fact, it is because there is so much disagreement to sort out in such little time that we need respect. It is even possible to respect climate denialists while knowing full well that our time is not best spent working with them.

We have all heard spiritual leaders talk about the need to respect and even love people whose behaviour we do not approve of, but the advice of professional diplomats and hostage negotiators may be more convincing to some tangibly minded readers. People in these roles must come to the best agreement that is possible with autocrats, criminals and terrorists, and to get results they learn to respect and empathize with the people that they must negotiate with. Acting as though we respect people is what most of us do, but if we are contemptuous of others, they can see it. The best way to say something convincingly is to believe it. The best way to treat others respectfully is to actually respect them. Trust the hostage negotiators and the diplomats: respecting people does not mean agreeing with them. You will, however, work better with those who you respect.

BUILDING COALITIONS, NOT MORAL SUPERIORITY

The need to be 'on the right side' is the deepest cause of our disrespect and discord in coalitions. If we remember that we, like most people, are likely to be wrong about something, it is easier to give up pursuing the victory of our viewpoint as our main goal, and to instead accept the messy task of finding our way to the least imperfect world that we can reach together. Delusion and foolishness are part of life, and we will not escape them. Our collectively negotiated action will be flawed, but it will likely be better than what inaction would bring.

Self-righteousness feeds a sense of superiority on one side and resentment and acrimony on the other. This is true even of self-righteous respectfulness and pragmatism. Avoiding the impulse to attack a person who we think has said something foolish and fighting the instinct to demonstrate our own intellectual or moral superiority by making a comment in a corrective tone or by offering long-winded explanations of the 'right' approach can all be seen as inner work. It is these tiny careful acts that can build a coalition.

RELINQUISHING 'OWNERSHIP' OF THE 'CLIMATE ISSUE'

As chapter 2 discusses, the cultural norms and sensitivities of progressive groups tend to dominate the activist space, and climate action groups have therefore tended to attract progressives. In order to build a mainstream climate movement, we need to learn from the people who have already been working on dangerous climate change and from others who have not. Nearly everybody stands to lose from climate breakdown, so a mainstream movement should be ready to make almost anybody feel at home. Accepting people as part of a climate movement without asking them to agree with climate activists about every issue is a sign that we are really serious about mainstream climate action.

JOY

We need satisfaction and joy to carry on. In fact, neuroscience shows us that positive feelings are the way our mind and body tell us to keep going. If our own reward system is not saying 'Yes! Keep going', then eventually we will stop moving. The drive of martyrdom only lasts so long, and joyless people do not set an inspiring example to those who have not yet started their journey.

We should remember that people listen to others largely because of the non-verbal bearing that they have – the impression that they make, as much as anything else. Being centred and happy is also the best evidence that we are doing the right and necessary thing. So to do difficult work it is important to learn to enjoy life moment to moment, so that we do not need things to happen on schedule in order to keep going. For that reason, taking care to enjoy what we are doing is part of activism, and (more broadly) of activation and action.

MEETING EACH OTHER AS WE ARE

Everybody has their own journey towards realizing and accepting the gravity of the climate and ecological crises. A coalition for building a better future will consist of relatable messengers capable of reaching audiences the climate movement has historically found difficult to reach. For example, we do not ask people to self-identify as 'activists'. (For further discussion of this point, see the dialogue between Anthea Lawson and Rupert Read in chapter 14.) In addition, we do not even need people to agree about the value of shared inner work. Rather, we want to help people to come to terms with the crisis, to identify ambitious useful actions that make the best use of their own talents, and to feel part of something larger. In this process everybody's beliefs will change; if our convictions about climate chaos are true and our plans are good, more people will come to share them – if we engage those people skillfully.

PATIENCE

It is hard to be patient given what is at stake. But we will have to be patient in order to meet people where they are. Moreover, this challenge is not going away: there is no time for delay, but we must nevertheless maintain composure despite suboptimal rates of progress.

For years I have heard people say: 'We have all the solutions, we just need to act.' Funnily, when you talk to the many people who say this, you find that all of them have a different solution. Imagining that everybody will just stop talking and act as one is another way of giving in to impatience. Politics and coalition building are hard, because though we agree on basic goals, our strategies for reaching them vary sharply.[11]

While many would argue that we don't have time for patience, it is already too late to avoid many bad consequences. Trying to deal with the mess we are already in hastily guarantees further failure. Truly accepting that 'this is a marathon, not a sprint' is part of our inner work.

BARRIERS TO INNER WORK

The impulse to strongly resist discussion of the inner work necessary for climate action usually comes from either (a) personal difficulty with making peace with climate chaos or (b) an aversion to telling others about the inner work that lies ahead. For most of us, there is also (c) a resistance to openly discussing inner work in secular culture, where discussion of inner life has historically been left to religious traditions that were considered separate from the public conversation. Mainstream arrangements for inner work such as support groups, therapists or twelve-step programmes have arisen, but they are often seen as activities for 'troubled people'. The biggest barrier to inner work for climate and ecology, however, is a lack of good first-hand experience.

Those who have avoided a difficult emotional journey with climate chaos have either not acted, have just started acting or are acting 'with tunnel vision'. Most people that we need to reach are in the first group, but the last group presents the greatest challenge to discussing inner work, because of heroic workrates and achievements without deliberate inner work. Typically, 'tunnellers' have abruptly turned their attention into climate action after a moment of intense climate awareness, seldom looking back. More often than not, this quickly leads to exhaustion, burnout or, potentially worse, a saviour mania. Some people find an obviously useful and paid role for themselves quickly and put all of their energy into it. Some experience little inner tension, but they are the exception rather than the rule, and nobody should feel shame for being unable to behave the same way.

Even for those who have spent a lot of time with the truth, it can be uncomfortable to inform others that accepting climate awareness often means at least some experience of profound fear, depression or despair, overwhelm or powerlessness. Also, this message carries a risk of scaring people off. But again we cannot avoid the fact that whether we warn them or not, most people will have to spend time in this difficulty. They will do so more effectively if they are prepared.

It is challenging to navigate secular society's taboo on discussion of inner work, but it is not impossible. One strategy for making inner work more approachable appears in the introduction to this piece: pointing out that inner work happens throughout life in common practices that we do not think of as inner, such as singing. High performers in all parts of life talk about the importance of inner work to their success, and a climate movement will have to be high performing to address the challenges we now face. Mindfulness, backed by science, has also challenged the societal taboo on inner work, and appealing to that as an example will work very well with some (middle class, educated) audiences as a way of establishing that inner work is practical. Other audiences will of course be put off by the same language.

The easiest way to address concerns about inner work is to offer an accessible form, such as intentional discussion of deep climate concerns, where people take turns speaking and others listen with all of their heart.

The need for broad social acceptance of inner work is why we should seriously consider speaking about it publicly, whether we describe it as 'resilience circles', 'support groups', 'climate awareness communities' or anything else. Public discussion is part of breaking the taboo, and it is a taboo that needs breaking. The more that people who have done admirable things for the climate emergency talk openly and positively about overcoming the difficulties of awareness, the more the taboo will fade, and the more people will do inner work to come to climate awareness more quickly, with less suffering.

COMMUNICATING THE VALUE OF INNER WORK TO WIDER AUDIENCES

The principle of meeting people where they are is of special importance where it concerns inner work. Many working in contexts of low climate awareness may wonder if the whole subject of inner work is inappropriate for their audience. But what about 'maintaining composure when facing up to climate change'? Or 'feeling the climate crisis in your gut without being overwhelmed'? Or 'not letting our differences get in the way of common hopes'? Accessible language can play a critical role in translating inner work for a wide audience.

Knowing your audience and having credibility is important for starting discussions about inner work, but as I have already mentioned, there is somewhere in everybody's life where they talk about the inner. Jonathan Rowson's 'Spiritualise' report for the Royal Society of Arts identified 'death (and loss), love, the body, and the soul' as topics that are widely considered spiritual even among non-religious people. So, accessible points of entry for spiritual discussion of climate are many: *loss* of stability and *love* for, for example, children or nature are two things that people consistently start to feel in their *body* as they contemplate the climate crisis, while taking action often sets their *soul* at ease.

We use the phrase '[shared] inner work' because it points towards a broad landscape that is important for a mainstream climate movement to explore. This short chapter offers only a small exploration of what is needed. (More such exploration is going on right now in the work supported and offered by the Climate Majority Project incubator.) This landscape of possibility cannot be captured very well in words, however: it needs to be experienced. Talking about the full extent of inner work to anyone who has not really spent time on inner work has obvious limitations. People who are not practising meditation, for example, can only experience the idea of meditation in an abstract way, and talking about meditation risks sounding intimidating or pretentious. For that reason, the Climate Majority Project incubator emphasizes the creation of a resilient and respectful culture rather than 'inner work' in its public-facing content. We must work to ensure that the need for collective inner work is perceived as the easy way into climate action, not as a barrier.

For many of us, after climate awareness truly 'hits us', a hope arises that, with the perfect wording, it might be possible for us to directly communicate what we have experienced, to cut through the walls of protection that surround insulated minds. We slowly learn patience. Though some language works better than other language, there is no magic wording. We should avoid replaying this dynamic with regards to discussing inner work. We have to be careful that we do not spend too much time playing with words in the hope of avoiding the hard work of engaging people who think and speak differently to us. Meeting new audiences where they are, while at the same time being brave enough to push boundaries skillfully, is simply hard. Accepting the challenges of these conversations is key to moving as quickly as possible.

CONCLUSION

Despite the awkwardness around discussing shared inner work, it is part of life, and when life's real challenges confront us, most of us do inner work. We might even discuss it with friends or tell workmates that a day off is needed, that we need time alone, and so on. A shift in atmosphere is created when normal people publicly 'go inward'. And that is an atmosphere that climate work belongs in. We can avoid the subject, or we can dig deep together.

Waiting for a messenger from the mountaintop should not be part of *this* inner work. A truly democratic, decentralized – distributed – movement would mean that we stop outsourcing awareness of our challenge to leaders and instead share this challenging responsibility together. Only then will we be able to create the next big thing together, by finding our ways to many smaller things. Only then will we have the resolve needed to bridge gaps that have grown over decades and centuries. Only then will we let go of some views freely in favour of others that make more sense. We are all in this great difficulty together, and the sooner we accept it, the sooner we will be a mainstream serious climate movement.

NOTES

1   See Bristow, J., Bell, R., and Wamsler, C. (2022). Reconnection: meeting the climate crisis inside out. Report, 4 May, Mindfulness Initiative/LUCSUS (www.themindfulnessinitiative.org/reconnection).

2   Due to the historic split that occurred between science and religion that we still carry in 'Western' societies.

3   See, for example, Hassol, S., and Mann, M. (2022). Now is not the time to give in to climate fatalism. *Time*, 12 April (https://time.com/6166123/climate-change-fatalism/). Tigue, K. (2022). 'Doomism' or reality? Divided over its message, the climate movement seeks balance. *Inside Climate News*, 17 June (https://insideclimatenews.org/news/17062022/doomism-or-reality-divided-over-its-message-the-climate-movement-seeks-balance/).

4   This phrase was made famous by Donna Harraway in her acclaimed 2016 book of the same name.

5   See note 1 above.

6   The phrase was popularized by Edgar Morin (the famed French systems theorist) and his co-author Anne Brigitte Kern in their 1999 book *Homeland Earth: A Manifesto for a New Millennium* (Hampton Press, 1998).

7   See, for example, Heidegger, M. (1969). *The Essence of Reasons*. Northwestern University Press. Macy, J., and Johnstone, C. (2012). *Active Hope: How to Face the Mess We're in without Going Crazy*. New World Library. Thich Nhat Hanh (2013). *Love Letters to the Earth*. Parallax Press. McGilchrist, I. (2009). *The Master and His Emissary*. Yale University Press. See also the works of Charles Eisenstein.

8   The Mindfulness Initiative's report 'Reconnection: meeting the climate crisis inside out' reviews evidence in favour of inner work to cultivate a motivating sense of connection to others and life on earth.

9   See www.themindfulnessinitiative.org/reconnection.

10   See, for example, King's 'Mountaintop' speech (available on YouTube at www.youtube.com/watch?v=HIhGhu3ZKh4).

11   See, for example, Roseberg, M. (2015). *Nonviolent Communication: A Language of Life*. Puddle Dancer Press.

CHAPTER 14

Active deterrent: can the concept of 'activism' limit the appeal of mass climate action?

A dialogue between Anthea Lawson
and Rupert Read

Activists are a vital force for societal change, but when a wave of *mass* climate action is what we need, does the idea of 'activism' and the baggage it carries prevent most people from getting on board? Anthea Lawson and Rupert Read discuss the pitfalls of moral purity and the need to move beyond 'us and them' attitudes, the better to achieve cherished goals. Complementary to the 'great "no"' of activism, they touch on the possibility of collective action that sets out to build new visions and alternatives directly: rooted in place and accessible to citizens hungry for change.

Rupert Read: In considering what it takes to mobilize mass climate action, I've been thinking about the barriers to entry vis-à-vis activism. Barriers like: feeling as if you maybe *have* to get arrested; feeling like maybe you need to be a hippie, or you have to be left wing, or 'green'; or feeling like you have to buy into an agenda of identity politics.

Anthea Lawson: We both took part in Extinction Rebellion: you were a media spokesperson and argued for it on *Question Time*; I helped block Waterloo Bridge in the April 2019 'rebellion'; we've both been arrested. Extinction Rebellion did something extraordinary in shifting public awareness of climate change, but we're both now looking *beyond* it. I'm not sure I see 'identity politics' in exactly the same way as you, but my enquiry into the ways that activism can end up perpetuating the status quo includes the same proposition you're considering: the possibility that the very idea of 'activism' is putting some people off getting involved.

RR: And that's really how the idea of this dialogue came about. To explore the very idea of activism, as possibly the ultimate barrier to entry. Maybe if we want an active climate majority, we need to get beyond the requirement to be an *activist* at all. That's what took me to your book.

AL: I wrote *The Entangled Activist* to explore the many ways in which campaigning ends up repeating and replicating the problems that activists want to fix. I'd been a journalist and then, working for campaign groups, I'd done investigations into oil companies, banks, illegal logging: environmental and human rights problems. Looking at who is responsible and using that to try and get policy change. Sometimes we got policies changed. Quite often we didn't. But I was starting to notice some of the ways in which we were using the tools of the system in ways that might help reinforce aspects of the system. The frame I came to, as a way of looking at all of these different ways in which we're repeating the status quo, is entanglement. Now it might seem a bit obvious that activists are entangled in what they're trying to change. But it's quite counterintuitive to the activist mindset, because we like to think that we're separate to everyone else: we're good and right and no one else has 'got it' yet. It's countercultural for activists to consider the ways in which they're part of the problem.

One of the examples I looked at was our entanglement with the people we are speaking to. We think we can just chuck our message out there and it will land, and we don't always think more carefully

about that. I became interested in drawing on psychoanalytic thinking about what aspects of ourselves we are projecting onto other people. I was looking at the projections that are going back and forth
between activists and the people who are hearing their message – let's
call them, for argument's sake, *not-activists*. In the moment in which
someone speaks or acts as an activist, a line is drawn, intentionally
or not, across which you're then seeing each other in a particular
way. You are being seen as the activist, and you are seeing the other
side as the person who is not the activist. That might be somebody
receiving your message, it might be somebody you're blaming for the
problem, it might be a person whom you're impeding when you're
blocking the road. I looked at what is going on in this interaction
and these projections that are flying both ways, and whether it is
actually helpful to what we're doing. And I interviewed people about
how they perceive activists and the same stuff was coming up again
and again. Being hypocritical, being righteous, being angry. Those
things are the cliché of activism; they're lazy journalism, but there
are also some truths in them. Righteousness is key, in its real meaning of defining yourself as right specifically in opposition to someone
else who is wrong. And that is a description of the dynamic that so
often occurs. Extinction Rebellion explicitly tried to say that we're
not going to 'blame and shame', we want to draw people in. But it
was still happening. Every form of activism I've ever done, whether
it's professional or grassroots, out in the streets or lobbying in institutions, there has been a perceived feeling, whether admitted or not, of
some kind of superiority. So that's where I think this enquiry meets
what you're saying, Rupert, about the need to have a much wider
movement that's accessible to more people.

   I'm encouraging us – anyone who's doing activism already, anyone who's thinking about trying to change things – to think about
the fact that we're not separate from the problem we're trying to
change, because there's this classic part of the script, which runs
largely unconsciously, where we identify the problem 'over there'.
We might have strong feelings about it that motivate us to want to
do something about it, either because we've been personally affected
or because we want to act in support of those who are personally
affected by it. But the problem is over there and we are separate, and

we make ourselves good by doing the activism, and that leads to a whole set of effects in how we come across and how we motivate ourselves and how we generate and maintain our energy – effects that are not helpful. 'Entanglement' seemed like a way of saying that things don't break down into these simple divisions where the problem's there and we're the ones who are solving it, we are the ones who are saving things. We need to complicate the 'goodies and baddies' story, to move beyond it.

RR: Yes, so it's about overcoming assumptions and assertions of moral purity. We live in an era of obsession with identity in the political media, in the form of identity politics. It's generally unrecognized that 'activist' is *itself* an identity, with a role in that politics, and it can be a problematic one. One reason I loved your book is that it expresses with great clarity some thoughts that had occurred to me for some years. In my years of activism in the Green Party (which I'm still part of and very much support, albeit less actively), I noticed that people would often argue for or against something on the grounds – implicitly or sometimes even explicitly – of what was *pure*. Of the alleged essence of greenness or what our irreproachable role was supposed to be, without the sense of a role for compromise in politics. And while clearly, right now, we need to be hyperaware of the dangers of corruption in politics, I believe that dialectic of purity, especially thinking 'we are the pure ones and those people over there are impure', should be recognized as very dangerous. It fuels the polarization that is tearing us apart. This kind of endless trend towards purism inside the Green Party took various forms including (increasingly) 'leftist' forms, and it started to feel deeply troubling.

In your book you express very clearly that ... as soon as we're inclined as activists to think we are pure and those we are fighting are impure, then basically we've already lost. You're drawing attention to the ways in which activism can create resistance and can be counterproductive. And then one can start to imagine how to mitigate some of those problems, as Extinction Rebellion tried to do. But I was left with the thought that, even if we could achieve that – becoming aware of the shadow in activism and so forth – isn't there still going to be a problem? The idea of activism is out there, defining even the most careful and most reflective activists in the public imagination. We have limited control over it, however we behave. I realized that maybe, as an activist who has been among activists for so many years, I've overlooked the way that for others, the notion of activism itself is unappealing; it puts people off the idea of taking action. The vast majority of people are just unlikely to ever get on board with something if it means they'll be regarded or labelled as an activist.

AL: I think a lot of people who do activism make an assumption that if someone is 'not active', then they don't care. I certainly used to. We have to look at what makes people activists. In very simplistic and crude terms we can say that some people do it because they are fighting for the conditions of their own life. They've had to turn to activism and there are plenty of examples of that. Then there is turning to activism from a position of conscience, but where you're not currently being affected personally by the issue in question. Environmental activism, in the UK, has to a great extent, historically, fallen into the latter version. It's not the only kind of environmental activism. There are lots of examples of people, often marginalized people, who are living in places that are more polluted and are fighting for the conditions of their life. But what will it take, in terms of climate breakdown in the UK, to wake more people up to feeling that they need to do it because they are under direct threat? I know you've looked at this in some of your other work, especially in your writing about children and care for future generations, which tries to bring that home. And yet we're still faced with the reality that it is not close enough to home for a lot of people.

RR: Absolutely. And that's an issue. We desperately need to bring home the vulnerability story: the truth, probably best expressed in narratives of actual and potential climate disasters that feel tangible. I also think that a lot of people are now concerned, and do care. Some of the care is thin. Some of it goes quite deep. A lot of people I encounter, including in business contexts, are really concerned, and they want to do something, but they're not sure what. And again, what if a perception of climate action as somehow *activist* is actually a key reason why they won't cross the value–action gap? But as well as asking, 'Is it really so bad being an activist?' (because of course it's not!), maybe there's also a strong pragmatic case for saying, 'D'you know what? What matters is not you becoming an activist. *What matters is you taking action.* If you don't want to be regarded as an activist, that's fine.' Actually, what we need in workplaces, communities and businesses is a lot more people to take action. And by taking action without regarding themselves as activists – with all the psychology that, as you say, goes along with that fear – they may provoke less counter-reaction than activists often provoke.

That is a central thrust of our theory of change (see chapter 3). Many people in their professions and communities, in religious organizations and so on, need to take action on the ground – to think about resilience measures in their local areas, for example, or to be willing to challenge their employers on commuting, or ask questions such as: 'What's your product?' 'What are you doing with your profits?' 'Is your supply chain resilient to shocks?' If that were to happen at scale – and it could – then that'd bring a lot more real change than we've yet seen. And the more that people take action into their own hands, of course, the more that governments can finally see how many people are really hungry for serious action – making them much more likely to act. We've had this historic consciousness raising with Extinction Rebellion, which I took part in, but the actual change, in institutions, through government, etc., has been a lot less satisfactory. The idea of the Climate Majority Project is to make it happen from the ground up – *and* the top down. What if the frame of 'taking action', or something like that, rather than the frame of 'activism' is actually the way that we can enable that to happen?

AL: Yes, and I think this goes beyond semantics. I think it's about where it's taking place as well. Let's say some movement was to arise – and there are people working on projects that might start blooming very soon; there are all sorts of things out there already. But if it is somewhere where people are not, and I'm not just using 'where' geographically here: it will still go into the 'activism' category. Which is why the point about workplaces is so interesting, and also about schools. For lots of parents, schools are where you have your locus of meeting people and sociality – around the thing that you are doing, which is looking after kids. Things that can be done in places where people are already, where they are spending their time and doing their work, feel less like they are this 'other' form of activity. In the research I've been doing, the people who are most likely to self-identify as activists are the ones who are doing the oppositional approach: the great 'no'. Whereas people who are building new visions, new alternatives, which often necessarily take place at a smaller scale because in order to actually build it you generally start in a community and sometimes you scale it – like the Transition Towns movement did, for example – these people are less likely to consider themselves activists because of the baggage around the word. And it's people like that, if I understand you correctly, who you are thinking of as the 'climate majority'.

RR: Yes! But I'd like to return for a moment to the idea of anger and oppositionalism. You mentioned anger earlier as a cliché that people readily associate with activism. Ask people to choose an image that connotes activism, for example, and you might expect them to picture a march with shouting faces and placards, rather than picturing people planting a community garden or something like that. There's sometimes a temptation in activism to choose feeling righteous, feeling justifiably angry, objecting to something, etc., over practical possibilities – perhaps even stronger possibilities – of actually changing things. As I said, over the years I've often seen purity prioritized over success in the Green Party. Sometimes we would rather kind of feel righteous and lose than have to in any way compromise in order to actually change something. Now: if you're more interested in objecting, or preserving your own purity, than in any kind of possibility of actually making a difference, that's a problem. Parts of the contemporary vegan movement suffer from this problem: from tropes of purity that are alienating in ways that can actually threaten the success that the movement does achieve.

Activism – especially in the environmental movement, but perhaps also more generally – is so often about: 'We're going to *go* and do something and make something that needs to happen, happen.'

Perhaps, in Westminster, or on an oil rig, or whatever. What I think you're saying, Anthea, is: actually, if you're 'just' acting in your workplace, school, religious organization or local geographical community, then that's usually more of a natural thing to be doing. That's going to make sense to an awful lot of people. And that's what we need: an awful lot of people to take action! The 2020s are bound to be a decade in which there is a rise in activism, which is inspiring. But if we stake everything on that rise in 'activism', we're almost certainly going to fail. What we need additionally is these much bigger numbers, who aren't keen on the idea of activism, to start to act where it's pretty easy for them to act. Workplaces are absolutely key because that's where most people spend so much of their time and, as Marx of course famously observed, have so much of their power. Mass action in workplaces could be an extraordinary lever and source of hope. For example, Lawyers for Net Zero, one of our key Climate Majority Project incubatees, is very much about an approach of action rather than activism. Senior corporate lawyers are very unlikely to identify as 'climate activists'!

AL: What's another word for action in a workplace? We have this amazing technology for that: it's called a trade union.

RR: There are consequential ways of taking action in the workplace – through trade unions, through professional associations, or simply through acting 'directly'. Another thing that I think is key is that people need a point of access that makes sense to them and doesn't feel like too much of a big ask. For most people, joining Extinction Rebellion – let alone sitting in a motorway or chucking orange paint around – is miles too big an ask. But doing something in your workplace – including, as you say, perhaps starting off with protecting your own rights (e.g. the right not to have to commute unreasonably) – well, that's not such a huge ask. And if people try to make these changes, and that action is resisted, they might well be willing to escalate a little further. They might consider short, symbolic workplace stoppages, for example; and that's obviously where trade unions and professional associations could come into the picture. It will be much, much easier to persuade people that this makes sense and is something they could do, rather than going out there and saying, from the top down: 'Come on, the climate situation's desperate, let's go on strike now.' We're talking about moving beyond the activist frame by lowering barriers to entry and making action seem more natural and easy: something that makes sense as an extension of where they already are and what they're already doing. Many more people may be willing to do this rather than jumping into the deep end as 'activists'. People sometimes say to me: 'We need a general climate strike now.' That's pure fantasy. But we might be able to get to a place where eventually it isn't, over the next few years, *if* we proceed in this kind of stepwise fashion.

To be completely clear, neither of us, here or in our other work, is saying that activism is bad, or passé or something. On the contrary, activism is more necessary than ever. There will almost certainly be more of it through the 2020s. The question is, will it be enough? And to that my answer is *no*. We need a balanced movement ecology and a menu of meaningful options – new as well as old – for getting involved. Ways of seeing how, along with lots of others doing the same and different things, in the same locale and more widely, if we're all very broadly moving in the same direction, that could actually make a huge difference. That, it seems to me, is an invigorating prospect. Circumstances will eventually drive millions to want action. It would be tragic if most of them were put off by the assumption that the only legitimate way of taking action was to become one of those 'activists'.

AL: We also have to look at how protest is being increasingly criminalized, with much heavier penalties, including custodial sentences, for nonviolent direct action.

RR: Yes. People are going to be more scared of full-on protests since the draconian anti-protest laws introduced by the Conservatives and backed by Labour. They need other routes to action. But we're also thinking somewhat beyond the concept of protest. It's very much my experience, recently, that more and more people are looking for something positive to do. One of the reasons why Insulate Britain didn't go down that well with a lot of people is that many felt it had a very negative energy. In theory, it was about something positive: insulating Britain. But it became about sitting in roads and blocking traffic. What I'm hearing from a lot of people is: 'We *know* there is a serious problem, and we want to actually try to make a positive difference.' And that could turn into a huge agenda in geographical communities, in workplaces, etc., that goes beyond activism as we know it. It's about actually doing the thing, taking the action that needs to be taken, and it's frankly about not taking no for an answer to a much greater extent than in the past. People are realizing this is about whether we have any resilient future; this is about 'whether my kids have a future'. That doesn't necessarily mean that they're prepared to get arrested, but it does mean that they want to do stuff, they want to do it soon, and they want to see how the things that they're doing can actually directly make a positive difference to the state of the world.

AL: I think that's really important. Otherwise most people aren't going to be doing it when the pressures of time and work and family are high. What you were saying about Insulate Britain reminded me of Joanna Macy's three pillars of the 'great turning', the move towards ecological sanity and justice. One is the holding actions – it's the great 'no' – and I think a lot of people understand activism in that category. Doing a great protesting 'No!': sticking your body to the road, or shouting your head off on a march. It's me with my suit on marching into MPs' offices and giving them what for. It's grumpy as hell, and rightly so. But the second pillar is the building new alternatives. And I think that's where a lot of people feel more comfortable. And the third pillar is the existential, spiritual underpinning.

RR: And this is one of the ways I think this kind of action is *more* radical than what we'd often think of as radical activism,[1] because it moves from this kind of primarily negative objecting energy into this much more positive creative space. And what I'm seeing and hearing a lot now is that's what people actually want. They realize that our so-called leaders are not going to save us, and they actually want to try to create that positive alternative system.

AL: I always want to be careful when I'm talking about anger because while it's useful …

RR: Absolutely. It's an energy, as they say.

AL: … it's not for me or anyone to say that anyone else's anger isn't justified. None of us know anyone else's situation. But it often gets turned into that type of shouty 'No!' activism.

RR: If it becomes an identity and if it becomes what the campaigning is all *about*, then it becomes counterproductive. It relates to this point about 'purity' even at the cost of success. Being identified as the angry righteous ones against the status quo can become more important, in a way, than actually changing the world. And that's why, in our efforts to build a climate majority, we strongly emphasize the importance of starting where people are, and then going on a journey with them. It's why we emphasize the great importance of genuine inclusiveness, which was an agenda that Extinction Rebellion strove to articulate but didn't in the end succeed in. We need to include people who will never identify as activists, people who are not willing to be arrested or who are scared, or whose politics differ from our own – whether that be on identity politics or on the left/right spectrum. If we're not interested in those kinds of inclusiveness, then the reality is that we're not interested in mass participation.

AL: And it won't be easy to do this, because 'action on climate' is not separate from politics; it's about what kind of world we want to create as we make the huge changes that are necessary. Questions of justice are going to have to be discussed. But I agree that a purity approach of insisting that we're 'not going to talk to those people' because we're so disgusted with their views is not going to help. I like the image of a fire, for the anger we bring to activism: if you've got loads of fast-burning fuel going on your fire, then you'll get engulfed. It'll take you with it: you'll burn out quickly and not have anything left.

RR: This is one of my concerns about where the youth climate strikes have arrived at. Justifiably, they are just so angry at chronic inaction.

I worry that this can lead to burnout. We desperately need a balance of emotions. The anger. The *grief.* The fear. But we also need the joy that feeds our determination. And – and above all, I'd say – we need *love* and care, suffusing it all.

We were playing with this term of 'recovering activist'. It is a sort of jokey term, but it does feel to me as though it has a little bit of truth in it. When I look back at my time over the last generation, and especially at the last few tumultuous years, there can be a lot of wounding in activism – and you say this in your book. And some of that's probably inevitable and some of it's even good. But is it possible that we could find ways of helping to lead and energize, ways of doing some of the stuff that needs to be done, that are a bit less tied up with anger, with a kind of negative resistive takedown energy … and a bit more about creating the new world. And then it might be easier to recover. We might have less to recover from.

AL: I feel like I'm having lots of conversations with younger activists, people in their early to mid twenties, who are feeling really burnt out by what they've been doing the last few years. I'm in my mid forties and I've been through a twenty-year cycle of my own with campaigning. And I also wanted, as part of the research for the book, to talk to people who'd been doing their campaigning for a long time. The important lesson I picked up is the idea of practice. And practice, specifically, as opposed to 'goal'. Now this is tricky. There is a paradox here, because of course we've got a goal! We've got some very clear goals. We want to survive. We want justice. We want a liveable planet. And there are plenty of sub-goals within that. And yet, doing the stuff that we do – and I'm calling it 'stuff that we do' rather than activism – with a strong attachment to the goal, and that incendiary energy, does increase the likelihood that we're not going to be able to keep going. Whereas somehow, holding the goal in mind and knowing that we are going to do what we can, we can last longer like that.

RR: In philosophical terms, a purely utilitarian approach is unsustainable. The approach we need is more Kantian/deontological, or virtue ethical. As you say, it's about the practices that you're following, or the kind of people that you're trying to be – the kind of self that you're trying to manifest along with others.

AL: That's right. I feel like a virtue ethics is closest to what inspires me to be able to feel like I can do what I'm doing.

RR: Me too. So, this has already been a fruitful conversation. But if this proposition really has something to it, then why hasn't it been discussed much before? You'd think that this would be the kind of possibility that activists or academics would have noticed, but as far as we can tell that hasn't happened very much.[2] Do you have thoughts about this?

AL: I think those are two different questions. Let's take academics first. In one sense they have looked at this, yet at the same time you could say they haven't. They tend to focus on why people *do* engage in activism, and you can read into the copious work on motivation to join social movements some of the ways that activism repels people. But it's rarely explicit, in the terms that we are discussing. And then the question is for activists ourselves: are we taking the aversion to activism seriously? I think the answer is largely (and with a few exceptions[3]) no; but why not? You would think we would, as we are in the business of communication: surely it's important to consider how we are received.

I think there are a number of reasons for this. One of them is the way that progressives and left-leaning people tend to be unwilling to look at the interior of human nature and use some of the insights of psychology. One reason for this is that it's what our culture does: we have a polarizing culture that separates the material from the mental.

RR: A lot of activists, for example, do *not* want to be labelled as spiritual.

AL: Exactly. Because, of course, we want to be serious about changing the politics and we're so focused on the politics. But I think part of it is the polarization of the culture coming through us. But others are looking at our inner lives. The insights of Freudian psychology were picked up by advertisers very quickly: the commercial world was using these insights from the 1920s in order to sell stuff back to us. The neoliberals are all over it. Thatcher once said: 'Economics are the method. The object is to change the soul.' You can look at it in Foucauldian terms and look at governmentality and the state creating us as the citizens that it wants in order to best keep the system going that those in power want. Sometimes it feels like the left, and progressives, are the last people to be actually looking at the interior of things. And looking at the interior of our attempts at change is what we have to start doing if we're asking: 'Well, *why are* people being put off by what we're doing?' For ten years, the gateway drug to thinking about the psychology of how our message has been landing is 'framing', which the Common Cause Foundation initiated in the UK, building on research about values.[4] Now others such as the New Economy Organisers Network and the Public Interest Research Centre are doing good research on framing.[5] Climate Outreach is doing it for climate communication, segmenting the UK population according to the messages that work for them.[6] And it turns out that, quite often, campaigners are putting out duff messaging. Framing is about the deeply held mental pictures that people have of the world, and you can activate unhelpful frames if you talk about, for example, migrants in a way that activates people's hostility towards them. It's really easy to get that wrong. So people are starting to come to that. But I think the deeper questions – of why is it that people are so put off by what we're doing and who we seem to be – are uncomfortable.

RR: Yes that's surely right. People don't want to face that. And, of course, we shouldn't exaggerate the reluctance to look at this question. There have been people who have done interesting and important work on this stuff before. Tom Crompton's important work is relevant, as is that of Chris Rose, George Marshall (who is working with us in the Climate Majority Project) and Bayo Akomolafe, with his post-activism concept. Extinction Rebellion itself, as you mentioned earlier, made this heroic effort to step beyond what would be, in the spiral dynamics terms, the sort of 'green' level to the 'teal' level, and to be genuinely inviting and non-hostile and so on.[7] But

I think between 2019 and 2021 XR gradually backslid into a classic 'green' orientation. It became angrier. It started erecting pro-identity-politics barriers to entry.

And, for me, the key explanation has to do with what you just said: activists' own discomfort in acknowledging these factors. Activists are busy, but also they may not want to turn the mirror onto themselves. If you're going to ask a question such as 'Is the concept of activism itself a key reason why what we're trying to achieve isn't happening?', that's uncomfortable.

AL: It also doesn't help that we have this pattern of valorizing and putting on a pedestal what is most 'activisty'. When I say 'activisty', I mean the stuff that we hold as the cliché: the big protesting 'No!' I've done some workshops where you get people to constellate themselves in the room according to the question, 'Do you consider yourself an activist?' One end of the room is 'definitely activist' and the other end is not. What happens is interesting, because people are not placing themselves according to what they've actually done. There are big discrepancies in what people have done and where they put themselves, which is according to *what they think counts as activism*. There are people who've done loads but don't think they're activists. Now the relevant point for our thinking about what a nascent climate majority looks like is, if someone says, 'yes, *this* is activism, and *that* is not', there is a risk that we don't see a whole load of work that is happening already. And we charge in saying 'right, come on, we need to start up a movement'.

I think that's why it's important for all of us to be really vigilant with our ideas of what counts as activism and what doesn't.

And I think that in order to maintain that vigilance, we also need to develop our awareness of what we've been seeking in activism, including that lovely togetherness. If we look at the alienation of modern consumer life, where we might be spending lots of hours working, and the culture has been turned into something where we have to pay money to do a lot of things, then being able to get together with a whole bunch of people and have some fellow feeling and do something that feels useful is amazing. If we have had to go against our family or peer group in order to wake up to the effects of business-as-usual on the climate, finding a community of people with whom we agree feels life-giving. It's restorative and that is obviously a really good reason to do it. But also we can get attached to the stuff that comes with the activist identity. And so being conscious of what is good about these things, but also what they are creating in their wake, can be helpful. Remembering all the while that the forms of *action* of which *you* are speaking, Rupert, provide that same promise of togetherness.

A final remark from me, then, about the sort of the activism that we want to critique; something about being on 'transmit' and not 'receive'. This comes back to what we said earlier about the importance of being interested in the emotions of those with whom you are in conversation. There's something about that being much more of a two-way exchange rather than us just sort of blasting it out there.

RR: And I hope we have modelled a little of that spirit of exchange here.

As we move deeper into a situation in which the 1.5 degree 'safe' average warming limit is clearly moving beyond reach, there are two possibilities for what we can do. We can get ever louder and more angry and negative and oppositional – which is just what the fossil fuel companies and governments and everybody else expects – and that will probably pave the way to, for example, even more oppressive laws. Or we can do something different, and in the Climate Majority Project we're recommending doing something different. We're recommending stopping and saying: 'Actually we need to acknowledge what has succeeded *and what has failed* amid what has been tried in the last few years. We need to be clear that we are in the age of consequences now, that targets like 1.5 degrees and net zero by 2025 are lost.' And then something very different happens. You're then letting go of various kinds of expectations that are baked into the system; you're opening up a space for those difficult emotions … and that can be so transformative.

And you're recognizing that a deeper transformation than we'll ever get from pulling technocratic levers or just getting oppositional is *just* what we need.

NOTES

1   See the postscript to 'What next on climate? The need for a new moderate flank' by Rupert Read (https://systems-souls-society.com/what-next-on-climate-the-need-for-a-moderate-flank/).

2   Emma Cradock's *Living Against Austerity* (Policy Press, 2020) mentions that some people find an activist identity and framing unappealing (p. 101), while her focus remains firmly on material barriers to activism.

3   Jonathan Smucker is critical of Occupy in this respect in *Hegemony How-To: A Roadmap for Radicals* (AK Press, 2017). See also Chatterton, P. (2006). 'Give up activism' and change the world in unknown ways: or, learning to walk with others on uncommon ground. *Antipode*, March. See also the 1999 essay 'Give up activism' cited therein, which can easily be found online.

4   Crompton, T. (2010). *Common Cause: The Case for Working with Our Cultural Values.* COIN/CPRE/Friends of the Earth/Oxfam/WWF.

5   Younge, G., Klein, N., and Stewart, B. (2018). *Framing the Economy: How to Win the Case for a Better System.* NEON/NEF/FrameWorks Institute/Pirc (https://neweconomics.org/uploads/files/Framing-the-Economy-NEON-NEF-FrameWorks-PIRC.pdf).

6   Climate Outreach (2020). Britain talks climate: a toolkit for engaging the British public on climate change. Report, 18 November (https://climateoutreach.org/reports/britain-talks-climate/).

7   Lawson, A. (2021). *The Entangled Activist.* Perspectiva Press. Chapter 7 discusses the application of spiral dynamics to activism.

About the editors and authors

Rupert Read is the author of several books on climate breakdown and a former spokesperson for Extinction Rebellion. He recently stepped down as associate professor of philosophy at the University of East Anglia to become full-time co-director of the Climate Majority Project.

Liam Kavanagh is a cognitive and social scientist devoted to using his understanding of human motivation, ideology and economics to aid more effective responses to the climate crisis. He is co-director of the Climate Majority Project.

Rosie Bell is a collaborative author and freelance writer, and a co-author of *Reconnection: Meeting the Climate Crisis Inside Out* (Mindfulness Initiative/LUCSUS, 2022).

Helena Farstadt is a chartered management accountant, a business consultant and a professional activist. She is Norwegian and lives in Norfolk with her family.

Chamkaur Ghag is professor of astroparticle physics at University College London and spokesman for the world-leading Lux-Zeplin Dark Matter Experiment. He teaches environmental physics at UCL and is spokesman for the Climate Majority Project's climate anxiety campaign.

Anthea Lawson is a writer and campaigner and the author of *The Entangled Activist: Learning to Recognise the Master's Tools* (Perspectiva Press, 2021).

Marc Lopatin is a former journalist and communications adviser with experience of the oil industry, politics and activism. He is the co-founder of PeopeGetReal.org.

Joel Scott-Halkes is Wild Card's co-founder and strategist. He is researching science-led solutions in land sparing and decarbonization, funded by the Quadrature Climate Foundation.

Joolz Thompson is a founder of iFarm (CBS) and Community Climate Action (UK). He works for Suffolk's Farming and Wildlife Advisory group helping farmers transition to sustainable agriculture.

Jessica Townsend is a writer, podcaster and social change entrepreneur: MP Watch is her third climate start-up. She recently featured in Josh Appignanesi's film *My Extinction*.

The editors thank Adam Woodhall, Ameet Mehta, Anna Hyde, Bel Jacobs, Ben Macallen, Carolyn Dare, Elizabeth Slade, George Marshall, Hugh Knowles, Jamie Bristow, Jessie Brinton, Jonathan Rowson, Kimberley Hare, Paddy Loughman, Rebecca Gibbs and Ruth Allen.